D0746271

WHY

MARGARET CHENEY

WHY-

THE SERIAL KILLER *IN* AMERICA

AN AUTHORS GUILD BACKINPRINT.COM EDITION

AN AUTHORS GUILD BACKINPRINT.COM EDITION

Published by iUniverse.com, Inc.

For information address:
iUniverse.com, Inc.
620 North 48th Street, Suite 201
Lincoln, NE 68504-3467
www.iuniverse.com

Originally published by R & E Publishers

Revised, updated and re-titled from the original book *The Co-Ed Killer*, 1976
edition, published by Walker Publishing Co., Inc., in New York; in Canada by
Fitzhenry & Whiteside, Ltd., Toronto.

ISBN: 0-595-08915-1

Printed in the United States of America

July 17, 1972

Mr. A. W. Girard
Collection Supervisor
Romer, O'Connor & Co., Inc.
703 Market St., Rm. 320
San Francisco, California

            Client: Beacon Oil Company
            Amount Due: $73.31
            Re: Edmund Emil Kemper III

Dear Sir:

    Your letter of July 12 has been referred
to this office. Mr, Kemper is in prison,
charged with eight counts of murder including
the death of his mother. The whereabouts of
his father is unknown. ...

            Yours truly,

            Office of the District Attorney
            Santa Cruz County, California

CONTENTS

FOREWORD

A PSYCHIATRIST, asked off-the-record where he would rate serial killer Edmund Kemper, III. on a scale of one to 100 "if 100 were crazy," replied unhesitatingly, "Oh, around 275."

I do not commend this book to anyone with a low threshold to nightmares. Kemper, like many serial killers, became a compulsive confessor after surrendering to law enforcement authorities via long distance telephone and began to pour out in meticulous detail his brutal and terrible crimes, leaving literally nothing to the imagination. It is a story so horrifying that veteran police officers, attorneys, journalists, and even psychologists were appalled on learning that the "gentle giant," who towered six feet, nine inches tall and was unfailingly courteous, could also have been capable of such monstrous acts.

The smart, manipulative young man is the self-confessed slayer of ten Californians: two grandparents, six female students, a friend of his mother, and finally his mother herself. Criminologists and gun-control advocates study him as a classic case, a paradigm of an American phenomenon: the serial killers now believed to be stalking innocent and unwitting future victims in every state in the Union. The FBI, which describes their sadistic crimes as epidemic, estimates that more than 500* such predators may be at large, often moving from place to place to avoid detection of their revealingly similar modus operandi. The profile of the episodic murderer is in many ways distinct from that of the impulsively violent mass murderer or from those who commit domestic attacks. The deeds of the serial killer are ritualistic, carefully and rationally planned, and compulsive rather than impulsive. There is seldom any question about their premeditation.

Like Richard Dahmer of Milwaukee who killed seventeen persons, Kemper had sex with his victims' corpses, cannibalized some of the remains, and kept especially prized organs as trophies or totems until they decayed. But, like the others, he had to be pronounced sane in the courts to get and keep him off the streets. As social commentator Art Hoppe of the San Francisco <u>Chronicle</u> wrote of the Dahmer trial, "Now that's crazy."

Medical science has moved far beyond the knowledge that inspired our Victorian law defining legal insanity, the M'Naghten Rule, yet we fear to change. Neurologists and psychiatrists now know enough to predict which children are at risk of becoming uncontrollably violent and alienated, and possible serial killers; they know how to help them before they are sucked into the black hole of vengeful fantasies and crimes against society.

Most such killers were severely abused as children, outcast, beaten down. Many have abnormal brain waves indicating

* Some data indicate as many as 3,000.

mental dysfunction such as disorders of the hypothalamus. "Repeated head injuries," says Dr. Joel Norris, a psychologist specializing in the study of episodic killers, "are one of the most important patterns for identification of individuals who are at risk of becoming episodically violent, even if there is no diagnosed brain malfunction."

They tend to be the victims of generational family violence and alcoholism, of drug abuse, malnutrition, and neglect. Many serial killers are highly intelligent, like Kemper and Ted Bundy, or creative, or gifted scientifically. As children, they are likely to commit arson, be subject to unusual problems of bedwetting, and be extremely cruel to animals. They dote on watching sadistic pornography against women, increasingly withdraw into sexual and religious fantasies, and often have learning problems or physical and behavioral traits that alienate them from schoolmates. The serial killer is usually a loner, although a few operate in pairs. Their episodic spells of uncontrollable rage may be like epileptic attacks in which the killer feels he has blacked out. As their fantasies center upon a particular type of victim, they become extremely careful and rational in preparing to strike. A cautious Kemper said of the women students, "I was the hunter and they were the hunted."

If serial killing is a disease, as some scientists now believe, a program of preventive treatment could save the lives of many victims and channel future perpetrators into safe and useful careers. But today's remedies, as in the 18th century when M'Naghten became the sanity rule, remain merely punitive and therefore ineffective. Such killers, on being indicted, are medically labelled sociopaths and psychopaths, yet found legally sane. On conviction, they are committed to Death Row or life imprisonment. The juvenile justice and adult criminal systems struggle to keep up with swamped dockets and the enormously costly trials and appeals. Most sobering of all, however, members of society remain in ever-growing peril. Nothing changes, nothing is gained.

The abused child is often identified by an alert school nurse, teacher, or doctor. Most abused children, of course, never become murderers, and not all future killers will have all the characteristics or afflictions, or the parental environment, described above. Society is rightly wary of stereotyping children who display some of the red-flag behavioral signs. Yet it is possible to make therapy available to troubled children without a stigma following them through life.

Kemper is perhaps the only serial killer to have requested brain surgery after his sentence to life imprisonment at Vacaville Medical Facility in California. Having brilliantly soft-talked his way past institutional and courtroom psychologists twice before his final sentencing to prison, he asked the courts in the late seventies for the right to psychosurgery "to stop the violence" and enable him to "become productive again." Although psychosurgery was once widely used to treat clinical depression, it was always highly controversial from the standpoint of constitutional freedoms, the danger of malpractice suits, and the general disagreement among scientists as to its effectiveness. On the other hand, forcing a prisoner to continue to live with his recurring violent rages when treatment is available might even be construed as cruel and unusual punishment—particularly since attacks on guards and other prisoners by violent inmates may result.

A convicted rapist in Maryland fought his way through the state penal system and federal court for the right to treatment with the drug Depro-Provera by Dr. John Money of Johns Hopkins University. The drug is said to diminish the sex drive to the extent that child molesters and rapists can be successfully freed of their compulsions. The rapist who went to court in this case had nothing to gain from treatment except peace of mind for he is serving more than a dozen life prison terms.

Kemper was denied the remedy of psychosurgery. Had he won his plea conceivably there might have been the danger of his winning parole on the grounds that his murderous rampages were cured.

Psychiatrists and neurologists, however, have made great strides in understanding the brain in recent years. Antidepressant drugs and related medications are much improved. As more is learned, it is even possible that delicate genetic intervention will join drugs as accepted modes of treatment, especially for disturbed children who show symptoms of future violence. Kemper's "little zapples," which he claimed he could not control, may one day be considered a clinical symptom. Various doctors have developed their own theories and names for the compulsion syndrome; and there is another rule of criminal law called the "product" rule: "Is this crime the *product* of a *diseased* mind?"

In Kemper's case, one psychiatrist was willing to testify in his favor under the product rule; but only the M'Naghten Rule was admissible in California and he was thus found *sane* and *guilty*.

The writing of Kemper's story was facilitated by the detail and compulsiveness of his confessions, which imbue it with the quality of a fictional narrative. His crimes are anything but fiction. My sources, aside from interviews with authorities and the courtroom testimony of medical witnesses, consisted primarily of voluminous transcripts of the murderer's taped confessions. I have quoted directly from such of the typewritten transcripts as were introduced in court, augmented by the direct testimony of Kemper and the corroborating statements of friends and relatives of his victims. In his verbatim confessions, he always referred to his victims courteously as Miss _____. The querying officials also referred to the victims by their surnames. I have elected, however, to modify the transcript to the extent of identifying the young victims by given names only and, whenever possible, have omitted their home communities.

—M.C., 1992

CHAPTER ONE

MANIPULATING THE EXPERTS

EDMUND EMIL KEMPER III pulled up at the curb in front of the Fresno psychiatrist's office, feeling mentally if not physically cool. The day itself was a scorcher, a blast of Indian summer from the furnace of the San Joaquin Valley. For a person accustomed as he was to the soft, cool breezes of the coast, it came as a jolt.

As for these little tests of cunning with the "courthouse psychiatrists," he expected to enjoy them. The day could, in fact, mark a turning point in his life. And if not that, it would at least inject an ironic touch to the game plan, a source of private amusement in days to come. Edmund had a special taste for wry humor. Anyhow, if nothing else came of this gambit, at least he would be keeping his options open. One side of his head told him that; but the other side said, You're a walking time bomb, playing with formalities while the seconds are ticking away.

Anyhow, get on with it. He opened the door on the driver's side of the banana-colored Ford Galaxie. The car's sheen was buried beneath dust and insect splatter, not just from the morning's long drive from the San Francisco Bay Area but from the hundreds of miles it had carried him in recent months up and down the state. He felt an affection for the hard-driven car with its crushed right rear fender and the University of California, Santa Cruz "A" sticker on the bumper. In a generally faithless world, it had stood by him. He hoped it continued to hold up. For Edmund Kemper had promises to keep (all vowed to himself), and miles to go before he slept.

Unwinding his enormous body from the car, he stood up and stretched. Even without stretching, the twenty-four-year-old man towered six feet, nine inches high. He weighed 280 pounds. A giant like his father. A giant like his mother. Yet he was a graceful giant who looked as if he might have been a professional basketball player.

Kemper wore his light-brown hair short and his moustache neat, which made him look somewhat older than he was. Even with the gold-rimmed granny glasses on his round eyes, there was a certain querulousness in his appearance that seemed odd in one so young. The eyes revealed intelligence and unflagging watchfulness.

He glanced up and down the tree-lined street and up the path toward the clinic. He flexed the fingers of his huge left hand. Edmund's left hand was used like anyone else's right hand, and at the moment it ached. Having the steel plate in his forearm was a damned nuisance.

Three months earlier he had broken his arm in a motorcycle crash and the doctors had put in a steel plate that measured exactly four inches long, and was attached to the living bone with six one-inch screws; and the bone fragments had not yet knit. The insistent pain made him even crankier than he might otherwise have been. Another person with a steel plate in his arm might have thought, Here I have this metal thing in my arm and it is about so long, and is screwed into the bone with a bunch of big screws, and it hurts. But not Edmund. With his I.Q. of 136 signifying "superior intelligence," he took pride in his powers of observation and in a keen memory for detail. He would have made an expert witness in any sort of court trial had life not reserved a more central role for him.

Before going up to the doctor's office, he walked to the trunk of the car and unlocked it. No one in the street seemed to be paying any attention. When, indeed, had they ever paid attention? This very human failing was one count in his indictment of the species, one justification for his game plan.

He raised the lid, peered inside, and adjusted some tools. He sniffed the hot valley air and found it reassuring. No problem. Smiling slightly, he slammed the trunk shut and brushed a smidgen of dust from his neat trousers.

Kemper entered the psychiatrist's office and the door closed behind him. A very short time later, he emerged. He was whistling softly. One down, one to go. Now all he needed was a "positive" report from a second psychiatrist before going to the superior court on his attorney's petition to have his juvenile record sealed. His attorney had chosen two psychiatrists who often testified as expert witnesses in the superior court.

The doctor he had just seen made a few notes. Soon he wrote up a brief report to be entered in the record, stating that he had examined Edmund Kemper. "I see no psychiatric reason," he wrote, "to consider him to be a danger to himself or any other member of society. His motorcycle and driving habits would appear to be more of a threat to his own life and health than any threat he is presently to anyone else."

The second doctor examined Edmund and found his mental health to be "excellent." He found him "normal" and "safe"; and believed with the best of intentions, without explicitly saying so, that the sealing of his juvenile record would help this bright, ambitious young man put wrongdoing behind him and forge on, perhaps to carve for himself one day a piece of that seductive old whore, the American Dream.

In their reports, the two psychiatrists were neither more nor less careful than thousands of their colleagues across the country. Someone had to take the calculated risk of recommending mental hospital releases, prison pardons, and court-record sealings. They were simply playing the odds that this former mental patient and criminal offender would not backslide. In today's state of the art, the odds against accurate predictions are extremely high, largely because no one can predict what stresses the released patient may encounter on the outside.

District Attorney James Hanhart didn't feel so easy about it. Personally, he thought the record should be kept open for another ten years at least. But what could you do? First, they had released Kemper as cured from Atascadero State Hospital. Then the California Youth Authority had paroled him to his mother. And now these two local experts swore he was safe and sane.

Superior Court Judge Jack Hammerberg did not like the situation either. He felt it was wrong to seal the record. But all he could do was rule on the evidence and that left him no grounds to hold back on signing the order that would make Edmund Kemper from that moment forth a citizen with an unblemished record. In the future when Edmund filled out an application blank for a job, there would no longer be double murders lurking in the past to cast a shadow over his neat block printing, no reason for him to check YES after embarrassing questions, nor even any need to incriminate himself on filling out gun permit forms.

Why, it was almost like being reborn.

Judge Hammerberg did not sign the order until November; but when Edmund came out of the psychiatrist's office that Indian summer day in September, he knew it was all in the bag. His lawyer told him there would be no problem.

Walking to his car, he went around to the trunk, meaning to open it. A blowfly was buzzing there and he changed his mind. Scrunching his huge body into the driver's seat, he started the motor and cut over to the freeway, heading back toward the cooling breezes of the Bay Area. He was driving hard as usual. Suddenly he started laughing. It was really something!

He even wished, as he often had in the loneliness of a private joke, that there could have been just one other person in the world to share it. Like little Aiko, the girl he had picked up the evening before in Berkeley. He had really been surprised when she told him she was just fifteen.

As he sped north along the freeway, he began to fantasize about Aiko, a girl he had scarcely gotten to know, and never would. But she was his now, for always. *His.* Too bad he had had to punish her, teach her a lesson for being so pretty and hitchhiking—as if the world were a safe place and a girl were entitled to do just whatever she felt like. They had no respect, these silly girls, for the dangerous arena where maniacal fiends worked their violent ways. (Edmund thought in the clichés of comic-book sadomasochism.)

The speedometer hovered at eighty. He glanced into the rearview mirror, found it clear of black-and-white Highway Patrol cars, and mashed his foot down on the accelerator. The dusty, yellow and black Galaxie responded. As always, speed filled him with a surge of power, erotic and beautiful. The world could beat a man down and walk on his head, but they just better not try to take his little old internal-combustion engine away from him. (If you asked him, the rotary engine wouldn't make it in the U.S. man's world. Too quiet.) His eyes behind the wire-rimmed granny glasses shone with excitement. It was a look one might see in the eyes of an arsonist watching his own blazing creation consuming a hotel full of screaming human ants.

Yesterday Edmund had been feeling "all torqued up," had felt the dangerous "little zapples" that he knew so well.

Someone always paid for the little zapples. But now the crisis was past and he was beginning to relax. Relax and enjoy!

He thought pleasurably of little Aiko's severed head in the trunk of his car. That would have to be taken care of as soon as he got home.

CHAPTER TWO

HOW TO MAKE A KILLER

EDMUND KEMPER, born December 18, 1948, at Burbank, California, grew up like almost any other red-blooded American boy, which is to say, in a home where the parents quarreled a great deal, separated, reunited, eventually were divorced, and where the mother wound up both caring for the children and working at a full-time job. He grew up worshipping John Wayne, whose image intertwined and blurred in his mind with memories of the beloved father who had abandoned him. He was taught to shoot at summer camp by a nice man from the National Rifle Association— "Teach a boy to handle a gun right and he'll never mishandle it."—and learned some lessons while a member of the Boy Scouts of America that would later prove useful, such as the proper honing and management of your knife, and how to avert discovery of buried objects by covering them with dry leaves, not wet ones. And later on when he was admitted to Atascadero State Hospital for the treatment of mentally and sexually ill men who break the law (more conveniently known as the "criminally insane"), he even joined a nearby chapter of the Junior Chamber of Commerce.

Herbie Mullin, who later came to occupy a cell adjoining Kemper's in the San Mateo County jail in connection with his own murder of thirteen persons, shared certain of these hallowed symbols and rituals with Edmund. He too had been taught to shoot a gun at summer camp by a member of the National Rifle Association. But Herbie possessed a creative brilliance, whereas Kemper's was of a more practical and utilitarian order. It was surely a great tragedy that Herbie happened to get off on drugs and develop the symptoms of severe schizophrenia. He was a promising youth whom his school mates at San Lorenzo Valley High voted the Man Most Likely to Succeed. Herbie recalled being *angered* once when his parents insisted that he go to see a John Wayne movie when what he really wanted was to go to a junior high school dance to meet some girls. And he later claimed that his long-suffering postal clerk father had made him a "killjoy sadist." Herbie's case is mentioned, as it will be again later on, partly to illustrate that no matter how you stand on John Wayne, you can still go wrong.

Edmund was the second of three children of E. E. Kemper, Jr., a six-foot-eight-inch electrician and his six-foot wife Clarnell. Both parents were heavily built and loudspoken. In good times there were rowdiness and joking around the dinner table, and these were the moments that Edmund later cherished.

Susan, the oldest child, was six years of age when Edmund was born. The parents called him Guy. And when Guy was two and one-half years of age, and huge for a toddler—bright, curious, and into everything—his sister Allyn was born.

His father, E. E. Kemper, Jr., had served in Europe during World War II in a Special Forces unit, which his son recalled as having included suicide missions.

The wrangling and shouting between the two parents found a new focus in the way in which Edmund was being reared. When he was four, his father went away for two years, taking a job in an atomic bomb testing program in the Pacific. E. E. Kemper, Jr., always claimed that the suicide missions in wartime and the later atomic bomb testings were nothing compared to living with his wife, Clarnell.

The boy's mother, he said, ". . . affected me as a grown man more than three hundred ninety-six days and nights of fighting on the front did. I became confused and was not certain of anything for quite a time."

"The war never ceased," Clarnell said bitterly. "Upon his [the father's] return he tried college under the G.I. Bill, couldn't get back into studying, argued like a staff sergeant with the instructors, dropped out, and worked rapidly into the electrical business."

She felt that her husband's work was menial. They argued over money and over the father's lack of attention to the children. Clarnell Kemper claimed that her husband was "stern to the girls and overprotective to Ed," saying, "He never spanked the children and they never had any respect for him. All he ever gave Ed was his medals and war stories."

When the boy was nine years of age, his father again left home. By this time it was charged that the mother had developed a drinking habit.

As the boy grew up there were always the mementos of battlefront gore and heroics around the house in the form of machetes, bayonets, and guns.

In 1958, when the father briefly returned to the family, he claimed he found that Clarnell was maltreating Edmund, having made him sleep in the basement for about eight months.

"He was terrified of this place. There was only one way out. Someone had to move the kitchen table and lift the trapdoor. I put a stop to it and threatened her with the law."

He also said that when Edmund was eight or nine years of age, the mother forced him to sell newspapers on the street, and that on one occasion the father went out looking for his son after the mother told the boy not to return until he had sold all his newspapers.

Clarnell, the boy later charged, was a real man-hater. Whatever the truth may have been on that score, she was persevering and married three times. (She told the social workers that she kept trying to find a suitable husband "because the boy needed a father"—a motivation that they cynically tended to discount.)

The boy's older sister may have emulated her mother's sometimes punishing rejection of him, if his recollections of various childhood incidents were accurate. (Versions of the facts tended to change from time to time, depending on whether they were being reported by journalists, expert witnesses, or especially, by the defendant himself.) He recalled that when he was about four years of age, Susan pretended to push him in front of a speeding train and in fact pushed him within a few feet of it. He recalled being, at the age of five, either thrown or falling into the deep end of a swimming pool and having to struggle to get out on his own, and he seemed to remember that he had almost drowned. In another account of this incident, it was stated that his sister had pushed him. It was also reported that she "lured" him into bed with her when he was eight and she fourteen.

At about this time he met his older sister's school teacher and confided to Susan that he would like to kiss her. Susan said, "Go ahead," but Edmund replied, "I can't. I would have to kill her first."

Death, sex, religion, and thoughts of suicide became confused in his mind at an extremely early age, swirling with the actual killing of animals and the mutilation of dolls.

When taken to New York and to the top of the Empire State Building when he was ten, he scrambled over the protective ironwork and had to be pulled down by his aunt. And even earlier than that he killed the first cat—to make it his—by burying it alive in the yard. When it was dead, he brought it into the house and cut off its head, which he stuck on a spindle and kept in his room. He prayed over it.

Once while still a small child, he went into a cathedral and prayed that everyone in the world but him would be killed. And later, many times, he fantasized wiping out individuals and groups. He thought of hiding in a closet and jumping out and attacking his teacher. One night, borrowing his stepfather's bayonet that he stole from his bedroom, he went to her house and stood outdoors while his mind drew exciting scenarios in which he killed her, then carried her off to make love to her. Certain women friends of his mother's were on his childhood death list; he kept track of their names and their changing addresses for years thereafter.

As a small boy he thought of killing men too, but he was not a killer of men, his grandfather's subsequent slaying being a matter of unfortunate circumstances, which he would gladly have avoided.

Norman Turnquist, Edmund's first stepfather, helped him for a time to overcome his death fantasies, taking him on fishing expeditions and teaching him to hunt. Yet even so there was a day at Hauser Dam near their home when the boy picked up an iron bar and stood behind Turnquist for quite a long time. His plan, after bashing him over the head, was to steal his car and drive to Southern California for a reunion with his natural father. In these years he thought continually of being allowed to live once more with his father, and made several attempts to do so. But he could not bring himself to lower the cudgel on his stepfather's head. Usually it was fear of reprisal by an older male that deterred him in such circumstances. All his life he would be a fearful giant who vastly preferred to strike weaker victims of the female gender.

Sister Allyn recalled that once she sat near him at home while he was cleaning a gun. Her back was to him. Suddenly she heard the splat of a bullet embedding itself in the wall of the room and the roar of the explosion. "Whoops!" said young Edmund, "I thought that wasn't loaded."

And another little thing he did that annoyed Allyn no end was cutting off the heads and hands of her favorite dolls.

The way Edmund remembered those years, "Very early, my natural parents were always loud and arguing, which terrified me emotionally of anything very loud and very pushy. As I was growing up, I shied away from loud noises and arguments.

"My mother was very strong and she wanted a man who was strong. My father was very big and very loud, but he was very weak and she wanted the opposite.

"You know, wooing and dating, you're one thing, but after you're married you let it all hang out. She was just too powerful. She would drive them (the men in her life) away, attack them verbally, attack their manhood."

The social worker's assessment of Edmund's mother was that she "seems to have had intellectual pretensions"; although why Clarnell's intelligence should have been interpreted as mere *pretense* when the interviewer had no knowledge of her capabilities (later she proved herself by advancing to a high administrative job at the University) was as mysterious as why young Edmund should have been described as "paranoid" when he reported that his grandmother watched and suspected him, which was no more than the truth and certainly a wise if inadequate precaution on her part.

After the boy's parents separated in 1957, Clarnell took the three children to Helena, Montana, and began a new home. She also found a job as a secretary at the First National Bank.

She and E. E. Kemper, Jr., were divorced in September, 1961. Two months later he remarried, this time to a German immigrant with a son two years older than Edmund. For the latter this apparent usurpation of his father's affections by an older and, no doubt in Edmund's mind, worthier son must have come as the ultimate rejection.

If his childhood in Southern California had been a frightening and miserable affair, a time of loneliness and confusion, which seemed to congeal as a glacial bitterness toward his parents and the world at large, his new life in Helena was equally tough and complicated by the added chaos of pubescence. He had grown up without playmates, withdrawing more and more into the strange constructs of fantasy. Now his peers were older and more in need of proving themselves with physical pummeling. Edmund had always been timid about competing in games and sports, always ridiculed for his size, always shy about sharing with other boys the usual conjectures on the subject of sex (his suspicions on the subject, while misinformed enough to qualify him for any teen-age gathering, being too threatening to speak of).

When the father left and remarried, Edmund had fantasies of protecting his mother. But a year later she married Turnquist, a forty-five-year-old plumber.

"I found out," her son recalled, "that she didn't need any protection at all. She used always to tell me how much I reminded her of my father, whom she dearly hated, of course."

Apparently there was never any intentional sex education of the three Kemper children at home, yet one of the most distinctive characteristics of Edmund that the psychiatrists brought out again and again at the trial was his insatiable, burning curiosity on the subject, which must have been present in early childhood. His second most distinctive characteristic was his keen powers of observation.

Dr. David Abrahamsen, a leading authority on violence in America whose theories we will discuss at greater length later on, writes: "To the child's mind sexual intercourse—the primal scene—is a bloody crime which, because it is secret, he is forbidden to watch."* Few parents realize the effect on their children of observing what the child interprets as a violent fight between the man and women in which the man, being on the top, is assaulting the female.

It is reasonable to assume that Edmund as a small child was inadvertently or otherwise exposed to some form of heterosexual overstimulation.

When ten years old he was involved in a homosexual act with a cousin—which in a more normal child need not have been any more traumatic than an eight-year-old getting into bed with his fourteen-year-old sister and feeling a sexual response, yet for him it was frightening. And there may have been other sexual exposures at an even earlier age, in which he was involved or which he merely observed, but with which he was unable to cope and found frightening.

* Dr. David Abrahamsen, *Our Violent Society* (New York: Funk & Wagnalls, 1970).

Parents may fail to realize the devastating effect on a child when one spouse ridicules the other or makes it apparent, sometimes obliquely, that the other parent is undeserving of respect. For a child has no model except his or her parents; and for boys, the Oedipal stage that occurs between the ages of six and twelve ought normally to lead to identification with the parent of the same sex. This occurs normally at the end of a period when the small boy subconsciously wishes to rape his mother and kill his father—and it is very touchy going for all concerned. If no model of the same sex appears as a strong figure, the effect on the child can be disastrous.

Dr. Abrahamsen, in his diligent search to understand why Americans as individuals are more violent than the people of any other developed nation, points out that the violent person has to demonstrate, particularly to his mother, that he is not weak. And since the U.S.A. has so much violence, it would appear that we have a higher percentage of weak people than other countries. He asks, therefore, what it is in the American environment that stimulates the mother's feelings about her son, "effecting a more dependent attitude."*

It appears to me that the reluctance of many American fathers to accept the responsibilities of acting as mature male models for their sons might be even more crucial to the roots of violence than a mother's feelings toward her son, since it leaves the son nowhere else to go with his dependent attitude than straight to Mother. And where American fathers do assume their role, many tend to confuse maturity with demonstrations of manly gun-toting and simpleminded asexual cowboy romance.

Dr. Abrahamsen generously allows that "the blame," if there is any, must be shared by both parents and in this he is more charitable than the average run of male psychiatrists and the lay public. However, no expert that I know of has suggested that the role of the father is even more crucial than the mother's to the young boy's subsequent development, particularly in the prevention of the sense of powerlessness and lack of self-iden-

---

* Abrahamsen, *Our Violent Society*

tity that lead to the acting out of hate. In short, what may be wrong with the American Mom's feelings about her son is simply that too often she is required to serve as the sole wellspring of any parental feelings toward him at all, and sometimes the well suffers from drought.

Clarnell Strandberg worried about Edmund's inability, when playing with other children, to "stand up for himself." And one reason she worried about the absence of a father figure for him to identify with was that a relative's son had turned out to be homosexual, a development that Clarnell ascribed to too much maternal affection and softness in his upbringing. Edmund's exile to the basement may have been a misguided effort on her part to make a "little man" of him. Throughout her life there were many signs of the closeness of their relationship, however unhealthy the symbiosis became. Edmund admitted that he was a "demanding" son even when he berated his mother most violently for her domineering ways.

At thirteen, he was accused of shooting to death a pet dog belonging to another boy in the neighborhood. Thereafter he was treated by other boys as a pariah, being taunted, intimidated, and chased even more than before. And he could expect no comfort at home from a mother who feared that running from clear and present danger might be a sign of latent homosexuality.

One day the neighborhood children chased him so threateningly that he fled into a nearby house, where a woman called the police in his behalf. Thereafter the boys became more subtle in their tormenting, merely spreading the word far and wide that he was the local killer of pet dogs.

On a warm morning in June of that troubling year when he was thirteen, he sat brooding alone in his bedroom where he had been sharpening his knife and his father's machete. His pet Siamese cat was sleeping in a chair. The cat sometimes angered him by not responding to his attempts to train it. It ignored him when he called it and seemed to be a spoiled, independent, arrogant beast. What was worse, it had recently begun to prefer the company of his sisters to his own.

Edmund not only felt rejected by a hateful world but it was obvious that, for some reason he failed to understand, he deserved to be. Something there was in his character that people and animals found revolting. Even in school where his exceptional intelligence should have won some kudos to support his ego, or where he might have been singled out as a potential athlete, he had discovered merely that left-handedness was an added cause for his differentness. In adolescence all children seek to discover who or what they may be, a search that will continue for years and in many cases forever; and one of the ways in which children acquire a sense of who and what they are is through the reactions of others around them. To Edmund, the concept was blurred, except that he was obviously a reject and a weakling and a big stumblebutt.

He longed to run away to his father's new home and become John Wayne's son once more.

Suddenly, without even feeling angry toward the cat, he picked it up by the nape of the neck, seized the machete, and slashed off the top of the cat's skull, noting with surgical interest that he had thus exposed the brain. The cat went into convulsions. Edmund, splattered with blood, seized a knife and, holding the cat by one of its forelegs, proceeded to stab it repeatedly in the chest and abdomen. He then became terrified at what he had done. Fearing that his mother would call the police and have him jailed, he picked up the dead animal, buried it in the backyard, and cleaned up the mess in his room. Parts of the cat, for reasons that he did not fully understand, he decided to hide in his closet.

The summer months dragged miserably by. But in the fall he was allowed to go to Southern California to the home which E. E. Kemper, Jr. shared with his new wife and son. At Edmund's request, he was allowed to enroll in school there for the fall term. But it turned out to be just like school everywhere else. Edmund's new acquaintances in Los Angeles soon became leery of him because of his destructive habits. The father was told how he would "sit and stare at people until they became upset." Edmund may not have known how he looked but he could see the effect this staring had on people. He was beginning to learn how to get his own back at the world without risking physical danger.

The second Mrs. Kemper began to feel extremely ill-at-ease with her dour and hulking stepson, now more than six feet tall, hanging around the house. She began to get migraine headaches. Once the boy happened to catch a glimpse of her nude in the bedroom. Later he recalled that he had felt sexually excited by this episode. And still later it would be reinterpreted, perhaps at his instigation, but at least by the journalists, as a sexual overture on the woman's part: ". . . the woman had appeared naked before him, using her sexuality to take his father away from him."*

He was in the Los Angeles school for only a week when at his stepmother's urging, his father sent him back to Montana to live with his mother and sisters. E. E. Kemper, Jr., told his son that he was financially unable to keep him.

During that brief absence, however, Edmund's mother had gone into his closet in Helena and found blood-stained clothing and the intestinal remains of the Siamese cat. She at once wrote, asking if Edmund had killed it. He then denied having done so.

The bitterly unhappy boy went home. But on Thanksgiving Day he borrowed his mother's car without her permission, drove it to Butte, got on a bus, and returned to Los Angeles and Dad. The father should understand, he felt, that it was his duty to support his natural son rather than his stepson. And besides, things had been impossible for him at home since that business about the cat and that other business about the dog.

To Edmund's joy, his father agreed to let him live with him. There followed a brief happy period which, in itself, was such a novelty that it scarcely surprised him when it came to a sudden ending.

At Christmas his father took him to visit his paternal grandparents, who owned an isolated farm at North Fork, a small town in the foothills of the magnificent Sierra Mountain range.

* Don West, *Sacrifice Unto Me* (New York: Pyramid, 1974).

But the pastoral beauties of the place were lost on the teenage boy. For him the farm came to seem like a prison or an old folks' home and he felt bitterly betrayed when his father left him there after the holidays ended.

For all the griping that young Kemper did, and later his continual casting of his parents in the role of scapegoats long after he himself was an adult man, (and taking into consideration the obvious shortcomings of his parents), it was nevertheless clear that both Clarnell and E. E. Kemper, Jr., made earnest efforts to provide their son with a wholesome upbringing. The father's efforts were sporadic but apparently motivated by affection. Edmund was sent to camp, taken on outings, given a dog and a rifle (the latter by his unappreciated grandparents), provided always with a home by his mother, tended by his resented older sister who understandably might have preferred devoting her time to her own affairs, and treated with kindness by his stepfather, although the latter was soon gone. Later on, despite the fact that his actions disgraced the family, the mother remained loyal to him through his darkest troubles, picking up the pieces, visiting him in jail and mental hospital, accepting him back into her home as a parolee. Throughout her life, he always sought her out, claiming on the one hand that she rejected him and on the other that she meddled and interfered in his life. He loved her, he feared her, and therefore he hated her.

For E. E. Kemper, Jr., the guilt and shame were too much. He quickly withdrew from all contact with his son, even taking the precaution of getting an unlisted telephone, being swayed in part at least by loyalty to his new family.

As for Clarnell, left to raise the three children as best she could and now disappointed twice in marriage, she was finding the world no rose garden. Society could not allow her to appear strong. To be strong meant to be domineering and for this, various kinds of punishment—both direct and subtle— would be inflicted. This fact (the woman's doublebind) was not lost on her intelligent, watchful son. All his life he would feel a righteous, Orestean hatred of *domineering* women, by which he meant any female presumptuous enough to match wits with him or even to merely attempt to sway him with sweet reason.

When Clarnell learned that her former husband had sent Edmund to North Fork to live with his grandparents, she started fretting. Finally she telephoned E. E. in Los Angeles in the middle of the night. He recalled that she sounded as if she had been drinking.

"That Guy," she warned him, "is a real weirdo. And you're taking a chance leaving him with your parents. You might be surprised to wake up some morning to learn they have been killed."

Edmund's father thanked her and tried to go back to sleep. Maybe the boy was a little strange, but he had plenty of reasons to have growing pains. Sometimes he wished, though, that the kid would stop thinking of him as John Wayne. Now he could hear his wife waking up and she wanted to know who was telephoning. She said she felt another migraine coming on. She was rummaging around in the bedside stand for her medicine. He got a glass of water in the bathroom and took it to her and then crawled back into bed. E. E. reached over and switched off the light. He wondered what it would feel like to feel like John Wayne.

Grandmother Maude Kemper, sixty-six, was a writer of juvenile stories and an artist. Her husband, Edmund Kemper, seventy-two, was a retired employee of the California Division of Highways who did a little farming now around their seven-acre place. To the lonely fifteen-year-old boy, this seemed like the end of the universe, his grandfather senile and dull, his grandmother another impossible bitch. What their feelings may have been for the sullen young giant foisted upon them will never be known.

Grandpa Kemper did his best to cheer the boy up and make a man of him, which is to say that he gave him the gun. He also offered to pay a bounty for every rabbit and gopher that Edmund shot with the rifle. He warned the boy, though, that he was not to shoot birds. Naturally, the temptation was too great.

"You never saw so many birds disappear so fast," Edmund recalled. "I was blowing them away so fast that birds started flying in a square just to avoid that place."

He was enrolled with no personal enthusiasm in the Sierra Joint Union High School in the nearby town of Tollhouse. Here the teachers found the six-foot-four-inch youth "quiet and cooperative." He never caused them any disciplinary problems and they were so grateful for this fact that it did not occur to them to worry about it. Thank God for small blessings. And the grades earned by the brilliant youth averaged C-plus to B-minus.

For a while his grandparents felt that he was making "a good adjustment," and he remained with them until the end of the school year in June. Then he returned to Helena, Montana, to visit his mother and her third husband, but after two weeks he went back to North Fork, arriving on August 12. The grandparents found him "sullen" upon his return. They wrote to his father in Los Angeles that Edmund had "backslid."

To the boy, it seemed that his grandmother was riding him. And he hated the thought of having to return to school at Tollhouse that fall. He felt sad and always wanted to be left alone. And when he got that way, as people told him, his eyes "got a funny stare." It just happened. But his grandmother, when she noticed it, would get mad and accuse him of doing it on purpose to worry her. She felt he was faking. She would threaten to call his father if he didn't stop it.

He had a dog there in the mountains as his only friend, which was one more friend than he was used to having. It seemed to him that his grandmother was mean to the dog, too.

He was scarcely aware of the fact that he was growing into a graceful, athletic-looking youth. His head with its light-brown hair was well-shaped, his small ears set close, his features even. And except for those zombielike fits of staring, his eyes looked bright, if unusually wary for one so young.

Sometimes he felt he ought to be grateful to his grandparents who meant to be kind to him, but the fact was that he disliked them and they made him feel uncomfortable. Why did they have to keep throwing it in his face about how much his board and room was costing them? He particularly hated his grandmother who reminded him of his mother and who "thought she had more balls than any man, and was constantly emasculating me and my grandfather to prove it.

"I couldn't please her. It was like being in jail. I became a walking time bomb and I finally blew."

His murderous fantasies had begun again. Once, pretending that his grandmother was sitting in the outdoor toilet—and you had to admit it could be pretty funny—he fired bullets into it and in his imagination filled her full of lead. Another time, as she sat outdoors painting, he drew a bead on her head with his new rifle. And the only reason he did not pull the trigger then and there was out of fear that his grandfather might be watching.

Much later he recalled with laughter how, one day, his grandmother left him at home alone when she and Grandpa were setting out for Fresno to do their monthly shopping, but she took Grandpa Kemper's .45 automatic with her for fear the boy would start playing around with it. And what made him mad was that she had already made him promise never to touch the gun.

But there she was, going out the door, and he noticed a betraying bulge in her black purse.

"Why, that old bitch," he thought, "she's taking the gun with her because she doesn't trust me."

In the wry way he had, he chuckled at the idea of telephoning the Fresno Chief of Police to report, "There's a little old lady walking around town with a forty-five in her purse and she's planning a holdup." And then he would give a description of his grandmother.

All during that hot, dry Sierra summer the tension in him kept building up. On August 27, he was sitting at the kitchen table with his grandmother, helping her to correct proofs of her latest story for children. Suddenly Maude Kemper looked up and noticed that the boy was sitting there with that weird stare in his eyes again. As usual, she took it personally. She told him to stop it at once.

He got up from the table, took his .22 rifle off the rack, and whistled to the dog. He told his grandmother that he was going rabbit hunting and strode out the door.

"All right," said Maude Kemper, returning at once to her work, "but mind you don't shoot the birds."

He paused there on the porch, breathing the hot, dry air of the foothills, heavy with the mingled perfumes of monkey flowers, California sagebrush, and pine. Flies were buzzing at the screen on the open kitchen window.

Suddenly he felt that same welling, explosive rage as when he had killed the cats. With them, though, it had been something that built up slowly inside him. At this moment on the back porch it just happened before he knew what was happening. The hum of insects became a roar in his ears. He quickly raised the gun and sighted on the back of his grandmother's head, eighteen inches from the screen, scarcely conscious of pulling the trigger. Blood spurted from her nose and mouth almost simultaneously with the roar of the explosion. He shot her twice more in the back.

The dog, whimpering in terror, ran off into the bushes but the boy did not notice.

He got a towel, wrapped it around his grandmother's head to sop up the bleeding, and then dragged her body into the bedroom she shared with Grandfather Kemper.

Moments later Edmund heard his grandfather's car straining noisily up the hill. It stopped by the garage. The boy, galvanized with fear, watched the familiar figure get out and slowly begin to unload groceries from the front seat.

He raised the rifle, sighted expertly and, firing as usual with his left hand, shot his grandfather through the back of the head. Now he became fearful that neighbors would have heard the shooting. He grabbed the elderly man beneath his arms and dragged him into the garage. Then he closed the door.

He uncoiled the garden hose, turned on the tap, and began to wash away the red foam until it soaked into the earth. If the neighbors came now, he could say that his grandparents had gone for a walk; that he had been shooting at gophers. But this was no real solution to his problems, as he quickly realized.

In fact, Edmund could think of no satisfactory solution. He was terrified. Sooner or later his grandparents would be missed, for they were not the sort of people to go off on a long trip unannounced.

As always when life became overwhelming, he turned to his mother for help, telephoning her in Helena, Montana.

"Grandma's dead," he said. "And so is Grandpa." It was the most frightening thing he had had to do, telling her how they had gotten that way. At first, he said it was an accident caused by the rifle's hair-trigger action but she quickly guessed the truth. And he begged her to tell him what to do.

On her advice, he called up the Madera County Sheriff's office and pretty soon some officers came out. They took him into town for questioning. After a while he admitted the murders, saying, "I just wondered how it would feel to shoot Grandma."

He had thought of killing her in the past, he said, but had always decided against it. He stuck by his story that Grandpa had been an incidental victim and declared that he had killed him to prevent the elderly man from having a heart attack when he saw his wife. Also he was afraid that his grandfather would become very angry and would either beat him with his fists or shoot him with his .45.

As Edmund tried to explain his motivations, he described the killing of his grandfather as a "mercy killing" in that it prevented him from suffering. Illogical rationalizations of this sort, alleged to spare pain to the living, were advanced for the first time that day but not for the last.

The newspapers carried a story with a North Fork, Madera Co. dateline, "North Fork Boy, 15, 'Mad at the World,' Kills Grandparents."

On the basis of a psychiatric report prepared for the superior court hearing, declaring the youth to be a paranoid schizophrenic, a diagnosis that would be heatedly contested in another trial several years later, Edmund Kemper was adjudged insane—a legal rather than a medical definition—and remanded by the California Youth Authority to Atascadero State Hospital for treatment.

The court psychiatrist reported that Edmund, after killing his grandparents and during a brief period of detention in Juvenile Hall, had thought about the lost opportunity of undressing his grandmother, "but felt that was an unnatural thought and did not want to talk about it."

He found the defendant "psychotic at this time, confused and unable to function. Has paranoid ideation, growing more and more bizarre. It is noteworthy that he is more paranoid toward women, all except his mother, who is the real culprit. He is a psychotic and danger to himself and others. He may well be a very long-term problem."

One of the many ironies in the young life of Edmund Kemper as it related to the criminal justice system was that, after killing two persons, he was found insane so that he could be sent to a hospital for treatment, but that much later, after killing eight more, he would be found sane in order to be kept out of a hospital for treatment.

The California Youth Authority is noted for its care and thoroughness in studying juvenile offenders' backgrounds before deciding what disposition to make of a case. Social workers and medical staff spent three weeks observing Edmund and some of them did not agree with the court psychiatrist's conclusions. One report showed "no flight of ideas, no interference with thought, no expression of delusions or hallucinations, and no evidence of bizarre thinking."

But it was agreed that he had poor ego strength, a fear of personal injury by other boys, and suffered from passivity. The killing of his grandfather was reported to be premeditated, based on a lack of logic. The boy's judgment was obviously impaired. And this psychiatric diagnosis—which also would be exhumed for use in the trial much later—was that he suffered from "personality trait disturbance, passive-aggressive type."

After killing his grandparents the boy said he had thought of committing suicide but rejected this, thinking that he could not "leave this mess for others to clean up."

On various occasions, he said that he only wanted to be returned to his mother and that he was living just so that he could eventually return to her. He expressed a great fear of cracking up and begged to be allowed to do this at home "and let others put him together again." A social worker concluded that his life was "tragic and almost hopeless."

A penal institution, it was felt, would only intensify the defendant's guilt feelings and would prevent his receiving the treatment that a psychiatric hospital could provide.

On December 6, 1964, just before his sixteenth birthday, Edmund entered Atascadero State Hospital, feeling understandable trepidation. But later he came to say, almost with affection for the place, that he had been "born" there. And sadly, this was in an important sense true.

CHAPTER THREE

ATASCADERO
EXPERIENCE

"THERE WAS A constant battle inside me that was the major thing of my whole life. I didn't have any social attitude, any social personality at all."

At Atascadero they ran him through the full battery of psychological testing—including the Minnesota Multiphasic Personality Inventory (MMPI) and Bender Gestalt. And before long, the observant teenager was familiarizing himself with both tests and testers, spotting their weaknesses and their strengths just as they probed his.

Here the I.Q. test disclosed his intellectual potential. For the first time in his life strangers began to take him seriously, adult professional people with degrees after their names. Some of them took a personal interest in him. They gave him a job that allowed him to develop self-respect. And he was told there was a chance he could be cured and released, possibly to lead a fulfilling life on the outside.

So far as most of the world knew, however, Edmund simply vanished for the next five years.

It might have seemed a curious choice on the part of the Youth Authority to send a fifteen-year-old into an enormous hospital (an entire community within itself) filled with convicted molesters of children, rapists, and adult sexual deviates of other persuasions. But when Kemper went there in 1964, Atascadero was an institution almost unique in the United States and great hope was held out for its success. Although a maximum security facility, it was designed without the guard towers and cell blocks familiar to prisons.

Had the teenager been sent to a prison with adult offenders, he would have been exposed to homosexual assults by the ordinary run of adult felon. In the state hospital, the most common inmate was the child molester, who is a notoriously timid sort of man. And no doubt Kemper's imposing size helped to discourage the advances of more aggressive inmates.

Dr. Alfred Rucci who, at this writing, is the medical director of Atascadero, describes it as neither hospital nor prison but a hybrid, "meaning that it is more vital than either of its parents." When Kemper was committed, only two other states had special hospitals for the treatment of sexual offenders. Now California alone has two, including Patton State Hospital near San Bernardino, which serves the southern part of the state, while Atascadero serves Ventura county and all of Northern California.

Peripheral security is high at his institution, Rucci says, to allow for great freedom of the patients on the inside, and he feels the hybrid has paid off.

"We have disproved the myth," he says, "that you cannot treat people psychotherapeutically in a confined setting."

The great majority of sex offenders at Atascadero are not insane or "mental" cases in either a legal or a medical sense; but the ordinary mental hospitals usually do not want sex offenders and, in any event, the modern trend has been to close down ordinary mental hospitals as rapidly as possible to the optimistic hope that cities and countries will develop their own treatment centers. In California the closures have had to be slowed down and some state hospitals have even been reopened. Patton accepts regular mental patients in addition to sex offenders and other special categories.

The measuring stick for acceptance of a patient at Atascadero when Kemper entered was whether or not he presented a danger as a result of his sexual sickness and whether or not he was deemed amenable to treatment. Out of one thousand patients, perhaps one hundred of those entering the hospital would have committed murder and another hundred would be confined for violent assaults.

A sexual psychopath as defined in the California system is "a person who has been convicted of a sex offense or who has committed other offenses and is found to have tendencies to commit sex offenses." Atascadero also accepts many self-committed men in the category of "mentally abnormal sex offenders."

Currently with 1,200 patients, Atascadero is so large that the patients and staff must work to make it tolerable. Dr. Rucci compares it to an Army post, a Navy ship, or perhaps a company town. "Without the peripheral security, we would have to have guards on the wards. But the staff is totally dedicated to treatment of the patients.

"A mentally disordered sex offender may have committed a crime that would get life—but here he may be able to get out in two years. So there is a strong motivation to improve. We have few escape attempts and little violence. Any female staff member can walk in the main hallways. If there are as many as two patients around, she is perfectly safe; although it might not be safe for her if there were only one patient there."

The hospital encourages government on the inside, beginning with elected representatives from the wards. Patients select their own movies, may picket the canteen if they think the price of coffee has become too high, and set up their own coffee shop outside until they get action; and insofar as possible they are encouraged to exercise the independence that they will need to cope with a complex world once they reenter it.

When Kemper entered Atascadero, Dr. Lee Sandritter was its director and the hospital was accepting only half of every hundred men sent for observation, returning the other fifty as untreatable, to be placed in a prison or another mental hospital. Of the accepted fifty, ten would fail to recover and forty would be finally discharged as no longer constituting a danger.

Of this forty, ten would be completely rehabilitated; ten would have problems, but would be able to maintain their equilibrium on the outside. Another ten would have more serious difficulties, yet they too would manage to stay out of trouble. At least, they would not be caught at it. Ten would repeat their offenses, for a child molester does not become a rapist nor vice versa. Thus, of the original one hundred men, only thirty would cease to be problems and burdens to society.

But this was still a unique record and far better than nothing. The terrible danger lay (and still does) in the fact that of those who seemed safe to release, doctors simply had no way of predicting which ones would be the repeaters. They were playing the odds with some innocent person's or peoples' lives —and they still do—taking a calculated risk as one does when one drives a car onto a freeway.

The other major danger in the system (and it remains so) is the lack of adequate follow-up. Until a released man committed another crime, his problems in the outside world would likely be ignored. A parole system was supposed to take care of this, but a parole officer was then loaded with so many cases that he could not hope to make a careful check on all his charges. (At Patton Hospital today, if a released patient buys a gun under his own name, they will hear of it—but of course it may well be too late.)

Edmund Kemper was sent to Atascadero when the acting out of hatred and frustrations was just beginning to acquire a certain social status in America, being contiguous with such worthy causes as the civil rights revolution, women's equality, and activism against the Vietnam War. Mass murder, assassinations, rape, and widespread violence of every sort became rapidly developing phenomena that exploited "respectable" social injustice and in a perverse way absorbed some of the social okay for the acting out of frustrations. Everybody who mulled it over discovered that he or she was a minority and was discriminated against, and everybody knew that the squeaking wheel got greased while the killer got, for a brief time, equal TV exposure with Hollywood celebrities, political crooks, and Mafia members. The French *invented* megicide but Americans glorified it—the worship of sensational killings that enabled weak men at least for a moment to claim the limelight.

And just as the massive personal (as opposed to political) violence sweeping America today was largely unforeseen in the sixties, many signs now indicate that the eighties will see far worse. Even the idea of what has been thought *normal* in terms of behavior has changed so rapidly that the lay term *crazy* becomes more accurate than the legal definition known as *insanity*, the latter being so irrelevant and archaic that it only confuses issues.

Dr. William Schanberger, who was director of the psychology laboratory during most of the period when Kemper was in Atascadero, saw him virtually every day. The director of research, psychologist Frank J. Vanasek, now director of admissions for Patton State Hospital, saw the huge teenager often and took a personal interest in his progress. The psychiatrist who treated Kemper regularly was Dr. Dorothy Pollock, who has since retired.

For Edmund, who had never developed a positive sense of personality and who many times experienced wild, uncontrollable rages, the central command post of his being was deeply buried.

"I found out," he recalled, "that I really killed my grandmother because I wanted to kill my mother. And my grandmother was worse than my mother.

"I had this love-hate complex with my mother that was very hard for me to handle and I was very withdrawn—withdrawn from reality because of it. I couldn't handle the hate, and the love was actually forced upon me, you know. It was a very strong family-tie type of love."

Dr. Vanasek, who works with great enthusiasm at his major research interest, was particularly interested in Edmund because he continued to be puzzled about the boy. His work habits did not accord with those of the usual psychopath or sociopath, which was the diagnostic category in which he was treated at Atascadero.

"He worked in the psychology laboratory," Dr. Vanasek recalled, "testing patients, serving as a crew leader in giving the MMPI and other tests. He administered a test that included a hostility scale, and helped to score it. He was a very good worker—and this is not typical of a sociopath.

"He really took pride in his work. Now, a sociopath would have been more likely to *use* his performance to achieve other ends."

Dr. Vanasek advanced a fascinating theory about the patient —but that was later on, when all that the Atascadero doctors could do about Edmund Kemper was a bit of Monday morning quarterbacking.

To some extent, of course, Kemper *was* using his work performance—to convince the staff that he could be cured. If he kept his nose clean, there was a good chance he could get out; but he must also have felt ambivalent about being cured and getting out, knowing so well how life was out there.

In Kemper's words, "I broke my butt. . . . I was the dynamic young man, and they began to say maybe we can let him out sooner than we had thought."

Meanwhile, listening to the other patients, as well as in his work, he was absorbing plenty of information (both straight and warped) about the subject that most interested him: sex. To say that sex *interested* him is a major understatement. Every aspect of it consumed him.

Listening to the aggressive rapists talk about their experiences, he began to have violent sexual fantasies. And with his slight understanding of normal sexual relationships, the assaults discussed by the rapists in which women were cast in the role of natural victims began to seem very culturally okay, not to say mind-blowing, even though he knew it was outside the law. What griped him was that, here he was cooped up in an all-male establishment during the years when a teenager was supposed to be meeting girls. The others all talked about what they were going to do when they got out, which usually was just what they had done before—play it stupid. Leave a witness every time. They would go on raping—or at least they *talked* as if they meant to, when no staff people were around—until they were caught again. In his own quiet, courteous, shy way, young Edmund took it all in and to himself resolved that when *he* got his own back on society, he would play it smart. There would be no witnesses. But that was scary stuff.

Sometimes the older patients approached him for homosexual acts, which he repulsed with fear and loathing. Yet it seemed to him that such goings-on were occurring everywhere, and once he was shocked by the sight of men engaged in sodomy in the chapel during the sermon. Participatory democracy, he felt, was being carried too far.

Edmund claimed, after shooting his grandparents, that he was a recently converted Christian who had always been interested in the Bible. When a biblical expression was used in general conversation, he always looked it up.

Although he denied conscious responsibility for his crimes, saying they had happened by some means completely outside his control, he nevertheless felt that he would be punished for them. He had recurring dreams in which his grandparents were attempting to destroy him.

And the biblical character with whom the boy most identified was Job, that much-put-upon fellow whose boils and trials are so graphically depicted. No one paid much attention to this association at the time, but later someone would.

Edmund not only felt that he had been born at Atascadero, but when he emerged five years later at the age of twenty, he found himself, as he put it, "an old fogy." Incredible social changes in the last half of the sixties had transformed the world he had known. The clothing that a young man wore and his hair style were no longer just clothing and hair but codes to a kind of behavior and a set of political and social attitudes that he neither understood nor could pretend to feel comfortable with. Society was divided and bitter, with students, blacks, Indians, and women all behaving like the defenders of separate armed camps, their common enemy being the Waspy old fogys of the power structure.

He came out square in 1969 to a world where it was chic to be hip, where acts could be kinky and things funky or camp, and where like everything was cool, man, and mellow, man, if you dig the scene, man. Where you been, man? In a space ship? With that short hair and that neat moustache, you look like one of those astronaut fellers, man, except you're too tall. And they wouldn't let a southpaw in one of those space ships, would they, man? So where you been, man? You sure don't look like a draft dodger.

What shook up Kemper, really angering him, was disrespect for law-and-order demonstrated by the smelly, dirty, disgusting hippies—and most of all, of course, the girls. He himself had always admired the "men in blue," and he yearned to wear a uniform, carry a badge, feel the cold hard thrust of a gun in his holster and a club in his belt. Imagine those hippies taunting the men in blue, calling them fuzz and even more contemptuous names, muttering "fuck off" instead of snapping to. If *he* carried a badge, he'd make them scatter.

As if things weren't confusing enough with everybody claiming to be in a persecuted minority, President Nixon had convinced the hardhats and blue-collars, men with whom Kemper naturally identified, that they as a "silent majority" had been too long discriminated against, deprived of the cream of the Dream, while being taxed to the hilt to support the frills of upper-middle-class youth and welfare chiselers. Little wonder that when Kemper later spoke of making his crucial decision to translate game plan into action, he spoke of "evening up the Accounts Receivable to match the Accounts Payable."

More than anything he wanted to get into law enforcement. Knowing he was too tall for the local police branches, he checked with the California Highway Patrol about their requirements. He was disappointed to learn that they too drew the line on height—at a point slightly south of his chin. He did the next best thing under the circumstances and bought a motorcycle.

It wasn't just that he wrecked the bike in a hurry that made him want a car. There were limits to what you could do on a bike. And no sooner had he gotten out of Atascadero than he had noticed that every freeway interchange near large cities was thronged with young people with their thumbs out. Even girls alone! He couldn't believe his eyes.

The hospital staff had told him they could help him to build some of the bridges he would need on the outside, and they recommended to the California Youth Authority, which retained custody of him, that he be sent to a halfway house. There he would be helped to find a job and maybe go to college. At night he could return to a "controlled environment" as every Rip Van Winkle should. And there would be arranged social doings where he could have a chance to meet young women.

In group therapy at the hospital they had done a lot of talking about how to establish good relationships with women once you had a background record involving a mental hospital or prison. But, necessarily, the talk was theoretical. Such as, how you handled the problem of letting a girl know (without letting her *know*) how inexperienced you were for your age and tremendous size. The whole prospect was fascinating and utterly terrifying. How do you account to anybody for the missing five years of your life? And what woman could ever fall in love with a man who had killed his own grandparents?

The hospital staff had tried to reassure him and he had sometimes halfway believed that it was all possible; but the other half of his mind kept its own dark counsel, knowing what it guessed, or vice versa.

The Atascadero doctors, in sending Edmund back to the Youth Authority, had recommended *above all* that he never be returned to live with his mother. And you wouldn't believe what the YA did.

CHAPTER FOUR

BACK ON
THE STREETS

THEY KEPT HIM for three months in the Central Valley area, during which period he was enrolled in a community college and earned straight A's—and then paroled him to his mother for another eighteen months.

Edmund knew this was contrary to the recommendation of the Atascadero staff, but the "family ties were very close," as he told the girl next door.

While he was in the hospital, Clarnell Strandberg, now with a third marriage behind her, had moved the family to Santa Cruz. A new University of California campus was opening there in a beautiful setting, an experiment with cluster colleges. She was hired as a secretary on the campus. Being an intelligent, hard-working woman, unafraid of responsibility, it was not long before these qualities earned her a promotion as administrative assistant to the provost of a college. Without the earlier pressures of unrewarding husbands and a troubled son, she now drank less. She made new friends, and handled her job very competently.

The youngest child, Allyn, who still lived with her, often babysat for the faculty families Clarnell met on campus. Among Clarnell's new friends was Sara Hallett, known as Sally, a somewhat older woman who was a University colleague. On the whole these few years were pleasant and interesting for Clarnell Strandberg; even relatively serene.

Santa Cruz, until the frenetic 1960's jolted it wide awake, was a slumbrous little boardwalk community made up mostly of the retired and the retiring. It was noted for elegant old houses in a style best described as Gold Rush Victorian. There were rose gardens, palm trees, miles of beaches, gentle weather. And these in turn attracted tourists to whom the town catered with seafood restaurants, gift shops, and cruise boats. A huge amusement park provided roller coasters and other ride concessions. Many tacky little cabins and motels, as well as flashy and more modern ones, clustered in the area above the beach.

The County of Santa Cruz, with its rural features—clean air, mountains, streams, redwood forests—had at first attracted mainly summer vacationers from the crowded, smoggy Bay Area cities. Now the spread of megalopolis was turning the summer cabins into year-round living quarters for commuters.

The lofty redwoods, with sun streaming down through their fine green needles, were conducive to hallucination even without drugs; but there was soon no lack of the latter. Good growing soil and easy living were an open invitation, first to the Flower Children and later to less innocent types. Every enterprising commune or solo Druid grew a patch of *cannabis;* but it did not end there. More enterprising men began to operate small, portable pill factories in the remoter parts of the forest, turning out LSD and amphetamines for the city markets, free of police harrassment. A small cult of Satanists from San Francisco liked the landscape and opened a local parish. After them came pretenders, exploiters, and hangers-on. The more sensational news media promoted the black-mass aura. Small sacrificial animals were occasionally beheaded, in part to mystify and terrify the elders downtown. The Charles Manson cult killings were much discussed in this period. Soon the drug trade and the feuds of rival motorcycle gangs began to result in a rash of violent deaths. Santa Cruz, as it had been in the recent "good old days," was threatened by the newcomers who filtered in from Hollywood, San Francisco, Berkeley, and points east.

The University was opened on a thickly-wooded, two-thousand-acre campus formerly known as the old Cowell Ranch. It overlooked the northern sweep of Monterey Bay and the town of Santa Cruz. Bright, hip students and young Ivy League faculty looking for a chance to grow with the institution were soon competing for places at the innovative school. The students were supposed to live in dormitories on campus and at first they joked about the poison oak being the Dean of Women. But many of them, after their freshman year, moved downtown to share slightly rundown houses or apartments, which offered more action and occasional access to part-time jobs. This meant (since no public transportation then existed) hitchhiking to and from the campus. Automobiles were discouraged, and it was a long, steep haul up the hill on a bicycle.

Almost before anyone realized it, downtown Santa Cruz began to look like a different place. New tastes and new merchandising ideas, bright contemporary shops, coffee houses, secondhand bookstores. An attractive mall lined with trees and flowers became a very pleasant place to sprawl on a sunny day. In this unisexual milieu, denim shorts tended to be frayed and very brief, legs tanned and very long, feet bare, hair worn carelessly. Students at UCSC, like those elsewhere, sometimes wondered whether they might not better spend the four years learning to be a plumber or figuring out how to break into the electricians' union, because it didn't look like all that many people were going to be clamoring for someone with a bachelor's degree in psychology, man. But meanwhile, another day, man, or miss . . . .

The women students of Santa Cruz were generally fresh looking budding intellectuals, unabashed about their scholastic
achievements. They enjoyed strolling in lonely contemplation
through the woods, sometimes trailing skirts of homespun,
linsey-woolsey fabric. They wrote poetry, conversed gently
with houseplants, baked whole-kernel bread, and gave
womanly thought to such provocative matters as nutrients and
nurture. In sum, they were learning to live in reason and harmony with a world where there would be precious little demand for either commodity, a fact which they had already
sensed but were determined to ignore. Most of them intended
to solve this dilemma, ultimately, by moving to Canada where
they would "live on the land."

Everyone—students, faculty, and visitors—when they chanced
to meet among the trees, smiled and greeted each other as if
all were Sunday hikers. But the students knew that in a very
few years this idyllic extended backpack must come to an end.
For two of them, the time was tragically short.

It was to this bright scene that Edmund Kemper turned, going at first to live with his mother in one of a cluster of looka-
like duplexes in suburban Aptos. Clarnell Strandberg's home
was 609-A and was painted green. Like all the others it had a
picture window. A high board panel screened the front of the
garage and the entrance to the little, walled rear garden.

The neighbors soon began to hear a lot of wrangling next
door, usually late at night, and the coming and going of motorcycles and cars at all hours. The huge, courteous, quiet, young
man who had appeared seemingly from nowhere to live with
his mother paused one day to explain these arguments to Carla,
a twenty-year-old neighbor girl.

Apologizing for the late hour hullabaloo of the previous
evening, young Kemper said it was merely the way he and
his mother handled things.

"We like to get things out in the open. My mother and I are
really very close, and we know these fights don't mean anything."

As he later told it, "My mother and I started right in on
horrendous battles, just horrible battles, violent and vicious.

I've never been in such a vicious verbal battle with anyone. It would go to fists with a man, but this was my mother, and I couldn't stand the thought of my mother and I doing these things. She insisted on it, and just over stupid things. I remember one roof-raiser was over whether I should have my teeth cleaned."

This atmosphere drove him more and more often to seek relief in beer and congenial company down at the Jury Room. This bar, across from the county courthouse, was patronized by off-duty police and sheriff's deputies. He enjoyed comparing notes with the officers about the merits of various kinds of guns and bullets, and sometimes he overheard them talking about matters that interested him very much indeed.

As for the officers, they were favorably impressed by his friendliness and respect—not like some you could mention. Not long afterward he got the Ford Galaxie and almost at once crashed the right rear fender and had to wire up the taillight on it. Many an evening he pulled in right beside a police motorcycle or a patrol car in the Jury Room parking lot; but even after one or two officers knew his background and knew there had been a little trouble over a gun permit application, not once did they ever ask to inspect Kemper's car, because you could tell at a glance what a fine, decent fellow he was. In the Jury Room he was known as Big Ed.

To one of his drinking companions, he confided that he had become engaged and he commented that a "man would be a fool to marry a woman smarter than himself." Kemper did not marry the girl. In fact she was seldom seen in the area and little was known of her except that she came from a Central Valley town, was small, blonde, young, and immature. Later he told an investigator that he worshipped her in an "almost religious" way and that they had never engaged in a sexual relationship.

In fact, he claimed that he had had normal sexual intercourse only once and this with a woman who rejected him when he approached her a second time. But he also said on other occasions that he had *never* had normal relations with a woman;

and again, that he had frequently attempted intercourse with a woman but had never reached a climax.

Even so, his ego appeared to be healthier after he came out of Atascadero. He had begun to think of himself as a not unhandsome fellow. He particularly resented the fact that his mother, whom he considered an awkward and ugly woman, kept introducing him to girls from the University who were awkward and ugly like her. She was always meddling, it seemed to him—that is, when she wasn't rejecting him.

Left to his own devices, whenever he got up the nerve to talk with a young woman, he chose one who was petite and pretty and neatly coiffed. He observed the many little things that a girl could do to make her clothing attractive even when she had little money. And he was beginning to develop a mingled fascination and hatred for what he saw as the advantaged upper-middle-class female, the free and breezy intellectual type who thought herself his equal or even superior to him.

It would have been a snap for Edmund to enroll at the Cabrillo Community College at Santa Cruz and transfer after a year or two to the University, where his intelligence would have assured him the same success and social advantages that he so resented in the élite. It was the status and power of a wealthy family background that he envied; but as a white, bright male in the California public higher education system, which is an outstanding one although it has traditionally discriminated in favor of the white male student, the stepping-stones could have been swift and rewarding. No doubt this fact had been pointed out to him by his mother. He must have known by then that for him it would be no great problem to compete with the normal college freshman. Perhaps he sometimes thought of getting a degree in medicine and becoming a surgeon, or maybe a psychiatrist. But making the effort did not appeal to him. Perhaps it would have meant living at home when he did not want to. Even in Atascadero he had been offered an opportunity to take University Extension courses. But maybe he sensed that if he dug in, worked hard, and made it in the academic world, he would automatically lose all those comforting scapegoats from the past—the unfairness of mother, father, stepfathers, sisters, psychologists, psychiatrists, agencies, institutions. Hadn't the California Youth Authority "turned him back onto the streets?" What did they care what it was like out there in that jungle? Maybe he would get to the books later. Say, a career in Business Administration. Accounts Payable and Accounts Receivable.

He took laborer's jobs, including one at the Green Giant Farms at nearby Watsonville. But it was not until he got the job with the Division of Highways that he was able to leave his mother's home and move to Alameda, a town near Oakland, where he shared an apartment with a male friend. But he claimed that she tried to interfere in his affairs even there, telephoning him and wanting to come up and visit.

"The hassle with my mother," he recalled, "made me very inadequate around women, because they posed a threat to me. Inside I blew them up very large. You know, the little games women play, I couldn't play, meet their demands, so I backslid."

The "system" was to blame for failing to cure him, and his mother for making him sick to start with. Somehow Edmund, even when he was twenty-three years old always found some power beyond his control to hold responsible for his acts. But with the time that was left to him and his mother, he tried to improve her personality.

"With my Atascadero learning, I kept trying to push her toward where she would be a nice motherly type and quit being such a damned manipulating, controlling, vicious beast.

"She was Mrs. Wonderful up on the campus, had everything under control. When she comes home, she lets everything down and she's just a pure bitch; bust her butt being super nice at work and come home at night and be a shit."

He wrecked the motorcycle twice, injuring first his head and later breaking his left arm, suing other motorists for these accidents. The Division of Highways gave him recuperation leave. After an out-of-court settlement of one case (woman driver), he bought the 1969 hardtop, two-door sedan. In it he installed a radio transmitter with a microphone on the dashboard (just like "Adam 12") and outside of the car he placed one of those snappy, attention-getting whip antennae.

With any spare cash he could get together, he started buying knives (there was one called the General that he kept razorsharp) and his first love, guns. The latter was tricky, though, because of the questions they asked on the application, and at first he just borrowed one from a former boss. He started driving a lot, picking up the best-looking and the smallest and the neatest of the female hitchhikers. Just to talk to them. But somehow, even then, he never mentioned it to his new buddies, all of whom were led to think him a fellow so adamantly opposed to trouble and violence that he refused to pick up a hitchhiker of either sex.

He was learning all the time, observing, perfecting his technique. Lots of times when he stopped for a girl or girls, they would peer into the car, see that he was alarmingly square-looking and therefore potentially dangerous, and would cannily ask where he was going. If he said San Francisco, they would often say, "Too bad. We're going to Santa Rosa," or maybe it would be some other town north or south along the California coast. But sometimes he might reply, "Get in. I'll take you." Usually they would say thanks and back off to wait for some filthy hippy with a straggly beard, driving a crunched old VW. Well, fuck 'em! Maybe he wasn't picking up as many girls as he wanted to *just yet*, but he was picking up *on* them. He was learning their weaknesses and how to handle unexpected situations. Pretty soon he even started picking up the girls themselves.

He covered a tremendous amount of territory in this graduate course. Most evenings and every weekend he was out there, cruising the freeways. You wouldn't believe the gas bills. South along Coast Highway 1 to Santa Barbara; north to the Oregon border. On 101 or new International 5, or 580 east out of Oakland, or old Route 99 down the Central Valley. But mostly right around Berkeley and Santa Cruz. Hitchhiking girls were everywhere and they were asking for it, tempting him, trying to lead old Job right into the paths of evil. He'd had it by now, letting the world walk on his head. A plan was being carefully perfected. And this time he, unlike the rapists, would not wind up back at Big A.

The fantasies he was enjoying in this period were explicitly megicidal.

"I had fantasies about mass murder, whole groups of select women I could get together in one place, get them dead and then make mad passionate love to their dead corpses.

"Taking life away from them, a living human being, and then having possession of everything that used to be theirs. All that would be mine. Everything."

He put a blue velveteen blanket into the back of the car. He bought and added some heavy, plastic garbage-can bags. He kept knives and one or more guns in the car. And all the while he was practicing the right things to say, the right places to stop, the safe girls to pick up, the safe weather. And he started wearing dark clothing on the nights he went cruising.

Later he claimed to have picked up maybe a hundred and fifty girls in the years 1970-1971—before it all blew up—and simply took them to wherever they were going, talking endlessly, teasing himself. Testing, testing. If a thing was worth doing, it was worth doing well. A rolling stone gathers no moss ... etc.

The number of pickups made by Kemper in this period varied according to whom he was talking to or his recollections at the moment or the current state of his ego. Usually, when not overcome by the urgent need to exaggerate, he said anything that popped into his head that would make him sound like just another earnest, troubled youth who had strayed from the paths of righteousness.

One day he removed the whip antenna from his car and looked the car over carefully. From now on there would be nothing about it to attract attention unnecessarily. He fixed the door lock on the passenger side so that he could slip a Chapstick tube into the slot while pretending to reach over and lock it. He regretted that crushed right rear fender and the Mickey Mouse job he had done fixing the taillight, but you couldn't always achieve perfection.

About eighteen months after his release by the Youth Authority and at about the time his parole to the custody of his mother was ending, Edmund made a determined effort to trace his father. For five years he had seen nothing of E. E. Kemper, Jr. Edmund, who always liked to keep track of the addresses of people who interested him, managed to trace his father through the electricians' union in Los Angeles.

The father would not permit him to visit his home but arranged to meet Edmund at a restaurant, thus sparing any worry to the second Mrs. Kemper. Edmund recalled that they spent several hours in the restaurant, boisterously drinking, eating, and catching up on old times. Since both men were huge, it amused them to pretend to argue loudly over whose turn it was to pay for the drinks, but in the end Edmund paid for them all.

"I knew he never had any bread. But we resolved all the psychic goodies, about the grandparents and how he had forgiven me and everything."

Then the two parted, and Edmund began the drive north. He picked up two girls hitchhiking in Santa Barbara and took them to their destination, but in his fantasies he was picturing how they would look without their heads.

Later on, some psychiatrists consulted as expert witnesses, noting that beheading could subconsciously symbolize penis removal, speculated on a possible link between Edmund's visit to his father, his childhood relationship with his father, and this particular fantasy. And then, too, it was such a short time later when he took the crucial step that his doctors at Atascadero had gambled he would never take again.

Clarnell Strandberg, giving in to her son's urging, finally got him an "A" parking sticker for his car, which she was able to do by paying a slight amount extra for her own parking permit. The same sticker system was used on other UC campuses, including Berkeley, which proved convenient. Strictly speaking, stickers were for the use of employees or students who had legitimate need to park near the campus buildings.

Sunday, May 7, 1972, was one of those perfect spring days when everybody in the San Francisco Bay Area seemed to be on the move—hiking, bicycling, driving. Edmund Kemper cruised along University Avenue in Berkeley toward the Bay Bridge, noting with interest how jammed it was with hitch-hiking students, hairy, dirty creatures slumped around every telephone pole. One man was kissing a girl while flagging a ride with his free hand. Disgusted, Kemper turned back toward town and cut over to Ashby Avenue, which funneled traffic onto the Eastshore freeway a short distance from the Bay Bridge.

He was wearing his "kill" clothing that day—dark jeans and a tan checkered shirt. His tan buckskin jacket lay on the seat beside him. Sometimes he wore his Junior Chamber of Commerce pin in the lapel of the jacket, but today he had left it home, feeling that it would be inappropriate to wear with the "kill" costume. Also it could be an identifying mark. But mainly it was just too fine to waste on these smart-ass girls, who had no respect for anything.

CHAPTER FIVE

HITS ONE
AND TWO

ANITA WAS ENJOYING her very first hitchhiking adventure in the company of her Fresno State College roommate, Mary Ann. They stood at the Ashby Avenue on-ramp to the freeway, holding up a handlettered sign, *San Francisco.*

Although their actual destination was Stanford University, an hour's drive south of the City, this would indicate to anyone who picked them up that they did not wish to take the Eastshore freeway that led through Oakland but wanted the Bay Bridge turn-off.

They were petite, attractive girls. Mary Ann, the worldly and sophisticated one (as the result of having lived in Europe with her family) was also slightly taller than Anita. She had

45

dark hair and huge blue eyes. Today she was wearing light blue jeans, a purple sweater, a purple felt hat, and hiking boots. She also carried a backpack containing a dress, a bathing suit, and an expensive looking German camera.

Anita, who wore round gold-rimmed granny glasses, was dressed in gray and white striped bib overalls, a red T-shirt, and a red nylon jacket. In her pack she carried a sleeping bag, a dress with embroidery on the hem, and a swim suit. She was a pretty girl, wholesome and sparkling, like a model for the Pepsi Generation ads.

She had never before ventured far from home, although she had longed to do so. The oldest daughter of a third-generation farming family, she was expected to go home most weekends. As often as possible when there was good snow in the Sierra, she managed to go skiing with Mary Ann and other friends. Her brother Fred also attended Fresno State College. It seemed to her parents a reasonably "safe" campus, and you could not say that for many of them in California nowadays.

As for Mary Ann, she was one of five children and had grown up in an affluent estate development in a town midway between Los Angeles and Santa Barbara. The neighbors included a few Hollywood celebrities and a number of well-to-do professional people who worked in aerospace, electronics, and scientific research.

When the family lived there, her father had been an engineering executive, but later he became international operations director of his firm's aerospace division. In 1964—the year Edmund Kemper entered Atascadero—he took the family with him to live in Wiesbaden, Germany.

For the next seven years the family fanned out to explore Europe whenever they had vacations. Many Ann attended a German school for a while, then spent a year studying in Switzerland. She became an expert skier, good enough to have aspirations, her father later said, of "somehow trying out for the Olympics."

With her in her backpack that day she carried a small address book containing the names of friends from all over

Europe with whom, her father said, "she held a very lively correspondence."

Throughout school she had gotten good grades and was usually a B-plus student. She had been on her high school debating team and won several medals. "As a matter of fact," her father said, "she went to the . . . finals during her senior year in high school."

Had Mary Ann debated less well . . . But, on the other hand, *not* being debaters failed to save the other girls.

Her German camera, her father added, had been given to her by her brother when he got a better one. "She was quite interested in photography and was trying to improve her technique."

The hiking boots she wore that day were expensive, too. Mary Ann really needed comfortable footwear. "She had recently had both of her feet operated on," the father explained, "and spent a portion of her senior year with both feet in casts as a means of improving her hereditary deficiency in her feet, so that she could improve her skiing. And she was quite solicitous of her feet because of the fact that she was getting over that thing. She was very careful to use the best kind of shoes that she could possibly get."

The scar on her shin, though, was the result of a broken leg that occurred in a skiing accident in Switzerland. "Her leg had been wired—a bone had been wired together, and then later the wires were removed. Consequently there were scars on her shin. Later . . . she sustained additional scars on both feet."

Wes and Gary, two boys with whom Anita had gone to high school, were the girls' hosts in Berkeley on Saturday night.

Susan, a student at Fresno State College, confirmed that they left to go to Berkeley to visit the two boys, and they also had a list of friends elsewhere in the Bay Area. "They were going to Stanford," she said, "to visit Tom Turney." In addition to their few belongings, she recalled that they had taken only twelve dollars in cash.

"Originally," Susan explained, "they intended to return the

next day, on Sunday. However, they phoned me on Saturday night at seven o'clock and asked me to get an assignment changed for them because they changed their minds and they were going to come back on Tuesday."

Wes, who was twenty-one, said they had slept on the floor at his place Saturday night. Sunday morning he showed them around the Berkeley campus with its view across the bay to the silvery profile of San Francisco and the Golden Gate Bridge, and Alcatraz and Angel Island. He had shown them Sproul Hall Steps, and Sather Gate, where the Hare Krishna dancers chanted to the beat of tambourines, where Brother Hubert threatened hellfire and brimstone, and the Intergalactic Pretzel Wagon dispensed earthly delights. They had strolled down Telegraph Avenue among the sidewalk clutter of every sort of huckstering, marveling at the electric energy radiated by the parade of students and street people.

On Sunday afternoon at around four o'clock, Wes and a friend drove them down to the Ashby Avenue on-ramp. The girls had turned down their offer to drive them to Stanford. They were in high spirits and eager to meet new people.

Afterward, as Mary Ann's father explained wearily, he and his wife tried to file Missing Person reports.

"We tried. We tried many places," he said. "First by phone in San Francisco and several of the other municipalities around San Francisco. Then I drove with my wife to the area, and we started at Berkeley and a number of other places; and finally at Berkeley one of the officers there had—one of the officers there during the night shift did take and file a report.

"We tried to file a report with the police in Fresno," he added, "and they told us—well, there is nothing to worry about, just wait; and they never did take a report. Some of them told us, since she was over eighteen, that there was nothing that could be done about filing a report."

(Parents just would not believe that the police knew better than *they* how it was with young girls. Girls ran away. Usually with boys. And this fact some parents just could never accept. Anyhow, with the new law, an eighteen-year-old was now legally an adult, and it stood to reason that an *adult* could not be a *missing person*. Just stop and think about it. And besides, the police had their hands full, everybody knew that. Harrassing prostitutes . . . Pulling in drunks . . . Why, if you put out a flyer on every girl who *ran away*, or sat around trying to memorize their descriptions, how do you think law-and-order would cope, and who do you think would have time to study the shapes of the ears on the heads of the FBI's Most Wanteds? But you might try the newspapers. Some of the underground papers ran lists of missing kids and tried to match them up with their parents. Or you might try that church organization down the street . . .)

Again and again in the rash of murders in the early seventies, parents encountered the closed bureaucratic window. The bureaucracy was getting its own back at the permissive parents, the mothers and fathers of all the smart-heads who had no respect for officers of the law. Let them advertise in the Classifieds.

Mary Ann's parents went from city to city. "Finally," her father said, "the Sheriff's department in Santa Barbara where I happened to be working at the time did file a report . . . Whether anything was done about it, I don't know . . .

"However, shortly thereafter, roughly one week later while we were in Berkeley, the officer there did suggest that we might possibly get the newspapers to publish a picture and a story, which we did—in the San Francisco paper."

Nothing in Mary Ann's character or previous behavior had led her parents to believe she would run away without telling them.

"Absolutely not. She . . . was at school and would go someplace for the weekends or what-have-you, but she would always tell us. She was in constant contact with us by phone or by mail, just about two or three times a week."

Anita's father talked of his daughter and of the efforts their family had made to trace her. She had been an "A" student and had made the Dean's List in her freshman year at college. "She enjoyed school," he said. "After two years at Fresno State, she thought of transferring—perhaps to a college in Colorado."

She had her own checking account at the Bank of America and a B/A Courtesy Card that enabled her to cash checks in other cities. Thus, although the girls had gone on their trip with only "survival" money, they could have paid for public transportation.

Anita's parents also tried in vain to get the police to help when their daughter failed to return home. The reaction was predictable, if one had ever had the experience before, but they had not. The set face at the pebbled-opaque-glass window (which threatened to be lowered momentarily), reciting the set speech; the straggle of troubled people in and out of bleak corridors. The rules, the policy, the boredom; and sometimes a warm, responsive face that truly wanted to help but had to think of the job and orders from the top. "You wouldn't *believe* how many people telephone us or come in here every day . . ."

"We tried all we could do to find her," said Anita's grieving father.

Finally her family hired a private investigator who spent another three months searching. His name was Robert William Heitman, and he spent several hundred hours trying to locate Anita, or even scraps of evidence about the manner of her disappearance. He used flyers and posters and newspaper advertisements. And all he ever learned for sure was that Anita failed to reach Stanford University.

CHAPTER SIX

"HAVE YOU SEEN THIS GIRL?"

AIKO WAS FIFTEEN years and four months of age. Slightly built, she gave the appearance not only of being older than she was but of being wholly Oriental, which she was not. At a closer glance one noticed that her long, dark hair was finely textured and had auburn glints.

The easiest thing in the world would have been for this teenager to have grown up emotionally scarred and bitter, for all the strikes were against her. She had been born illegitimate, female, and Eurasian in a low-income household where her only models were elderly immigrant grandparents and her working mother. By the social norms that predict human misery, she should have been a moping, ego-deprived girl with little hope of leading a fulfilling life. The fact that both her morale and expectations were buoyant was a tribute to her strong, proud, and intelligent mother.

The girl lived with her Latvian mother and maternal grandparents in a lower-class residential section of Berkeley. The mother, for Aiko's sake, had taken the name of the child's Korean father.

The grandfather, after coming to the United States, had worked for ten years and now received Social Security. The old couple's income helped to stretch the earnings of the mother in her job as a foreign-language cataloguer in the University of California library.

Aiko, from the age of four, had been given lessons in classical dancing, both ballet and Korean, and her teachers thought she had talent. Her mother, by dint of unusual scrimping and saving, was able to send her daughter to the Anna Head School in Oakland, the best private school in the East Bay. And the child, justifying this commitment, helped to pay her way by earning scholarships. At fifteen she was, as everyone thought, on her way to a promising career as a classical dancer.

"Her father deserted us before she was born," the mother said. "He promised to help but he did not. He forgot about it." And she had never asked him for help, saying, "So I felt that if he did not like us . . ." She shrugged.

"I wanted my daughter. And I raised her with what I earned. I have worked for fourteen years for the University. . . . I told them that I had been married and divorced, or else I would not have been hired. I would not have been able to support her."

The costs of education had ruled out acquiring most of the material things normally considered essential to growing up whole in America. For example, there had never been a family automobile and Aiko had seldom even ridden in one. The costumes needed for her dance recitals were made by her mother. In addition there had been the cost of piano lessons.

Aiko herself had just begun to earn a little money.

"Aiko earned one hundred dollars from her performances," her mother said. "She did eighteen public performances since she was nine until the time she has—she disappeared; and we have a list, which I compiled after she disappeared, of her performances; and we have a book with programs where her name is printed on the programs, and thank-you letters, and also newspaper clippings in which her pictures appeared quite frequently while she performed. As a Korean dancer, she was considered almost professional. We have colored movies . . ."

But even though thousands of dollars had been spent on Aiko's careful education, the mother made it clear, "We didn't do it for money. We did it because it is—it established my daughter as a person, as a dancer, and it made us all good. And —and we had much joy out of it."

Because public transportation to San Francisco across the Bay was expensive for one of her means, Aiko studied at a Berkeley dance studio.

On the evening of September 14, 1972, however, she was invited to attend a class in advanced dance at a San Francisco studio. For her this represented an exciting glimpse of what she hoped the future might promise, and she left the house at seven o'clock sharp.

"We know the time, because my daughter asked for bus money from my father. That's the time when a certain television news program was going off. We know when she was seen at the bus stop, because some neighbors were going to a movie and saw her talking to a girl, waiting for the bus."

When Aiko left the house she was wearing brown corduroy slacks and a green turtleneck sweater, a denim jacket, and a hat of black velvet. She carried a faded Greek bag which was blue with a white pattern. In the bag were her school Latin book, a pink comb, a tiny dance costume. She also had a white woolen scarf which her mother had given her the previous summer. The only money she carried, which was just enough for the bus, was the dollar her grandfather gave her.

While waiting for the bus at the corner of Shattuck and University Avenues, she fell into conversation with a girl named Ann.

Ann recalled, "She told me she was going to San Francisco to a dance class and that she was waiting for a bus. We talked for about five minutes—about her family, school, things like that."

She added that she had been surprised to learn that Aiko was only fifteen, saying she had looked "much, much older."

But Ann did not learn the other girl's name until later, after seeing a picture of her on a telephone pole on University Avenue. Underneath the picture was a question: "Have you seen this girl?" Ann at once telephoned the Berkeley Police Department. Because she remembered that Aiko had not caught the bus that night.

"She got tired of waiting," Ann said, "and decided to hitch-hike."

Ann saw Aiko catch a ride. She described the car as "A cream or tan-colored sedan, late sixty model." (Kemper's car was usually caked with mud and dust from his travels.) Driving the car had been, "A fairly tall male Caucasian with light brown, medium brown hair. That is the best description I can give."

When Aiko failed to return home by eleven o'clock that night, her mother began to worry. She telephoned first to the dance studio and learned that her daughter had never arrived. Between midnight and 1 o'clock she communicated with the Berkeley police and reported Aiko missing.

She and friends of the family made posters which they pasted up all over Berkeley. They notified all the newspapers. They stood by buses, night after night, asking strangers over and over if they had seen the girl in the photo boarding a bus. Then, after Ann told what she had seen, they turned to other measures.

"I wrote to some—all—the small police departments in California, Oregon, and Washington," the girl's mother said. "I wrote to communes across the country and throughout California, and I contacted the FBI. I guess that's about it."

Aiko would never have run away without telling her, she insisted. She had been a happy girl— "as far as can be."

But the girl who had managed to rise above everything that a patriarchal society had sought to put her down with could not return home again. The mementos of her ephemeral passage, the dance programs, photos, color movies, clippings, costumes, and childhood toys, together with the remembered joy of her presence, were all that remained to the three human beings who, night after night, tuned in the evening news.

CHAPTER SEVEN

DEATH IN DREAMSVILLE

IN 1970 THE Santa Cruz area began to acquire a notoriety that could no longer be attributed to hippies. John Linley Frazier, the first of three mass murderers to strike in as many years, was in fact reported to the sheriff as a murder suspect by members of a local experiment-in-living group. To Santa Cruz crime buffs he soon became known as the Ding-Dong, Avon-Calling killer.

God told him (according to Frazier's version of their relationship) to call at every house, speak only to the man of the family, and with him, decide whether the rest of the family should live or die. Perhaps they might decide to kill all the others and destroy the family possessions. But in any event, the two chosen men would then join God and proceed on to the next house. Only in American Dreamsville could such a heady brew of male authoritarianism and religious fervor, well stirred in the mind of a drug freak, have seemed so easily possible of achievement.

At house No. 2 the chosen men would again confer only with the male head-of-household, and with God's blessing, decide on the fates of the lesser members, the women, children, retainers, and household pets.

Thus Dr. Victor Ohta, an eye surgeon of Japanese descent, returned to his beautiful country home one afternoon to find his wife, two children, and his secretary tied up and terrorized by the drug-and-power-crazed Frazier. Dr. Ohta mistakenly resisted Frazier's invitation to join him in the holy mission. Frazier threw him into the swimming pool. Dr. Ohta tried to pull Frazier in too, but the latter overpowered and drowned him. Had Ohta realized that his attacker had the strength of all the prophets of the Old Testament on his side, lending righteousness to drug-madness, he might have given in and in so doing have saved at least his own life. As it was, Frazier proceeded to shoot the lesser mortals as soon as he had finished with the doctor.

Frazier's wife and friends had tried unsuccessfully to get him committed to a mental institution or a drug treatment center prior to this final murderous outburst. But he always managed to give them the slip. He was tried, and a jury, finding him *sane*, convicted him of five counts of murder.

But random killings continued to plague the Santa Cruz area. The mutilated body of Fred Bennett, captain of the Oakland Black Panthers, was found scattered across the slopes of Loma Prieta. Law enforcement people believed he had been executed while hiding out in a woodsy bomb factory. On up the coast, the victims of motorcycle-gang killings, both male and female, turned up. And women students vanished, some never to be found. At the same time bodies, never to be identified, occasionally turned up, these being long decomposed.

At first no one connected the disappearances of Mary Ann, Anita, or Aiko with the Santa Cruz scene. Then a Cabrillo Community College girl named Mary disappeared and was not seen again.

It became obvious that one or more murderers, at least *one* with a decided skill for dissection, was working in the Santa Cruz area. And it became more obvious as more bodies washed up in the surf or were discovered in the hills. The pure randomness of the killings plus continuing reports of rape terrorized and angered the community. So far as women students were concerned, it could as well be one as another who was "hit" next. What could you do except try not to hitch rides and keep your door locked?

A women's group, newly formed, picketed the county jail to protest that rape cases were receiving too little active concern on the part of law enforcement officers. The sheriff's office then issued a warning to hitchhikers: "Ten rapes, eight assaults with intent to commit rape, three incidents of indecent exposure, two kidnappings, and one incident of sex perversion. That's 24 cases in 1972 in the unincorporated area of Santa Cruz county —all connected with hitchhiking."

A special Rape Line telephone number was installed in public telephone booths downtown, creating a rather ugly note in the normally sunny and relaxed mall. Two women organized the local group to fight rape, which included a counseling service for victims.

The University, besieged by worried parents and concerned that enrollments were dropping, which they were, took certain steps. Bulletin boards warned:

"When possible, girls especially, stay in dorms after midnight with doors locked.

"If you must be out at night—walk in pairs.

"DON'T HITCH A RIDE, PLEASE! If you feel you must hitch a ride—do it with a friend, but NOT ALONE. Try to choose cars with University parking decals (A, B, C or R)."

It was easier to caution students not to hitch rides, however, than for them to stop doing it. The previous year, they had started a cooperative program with the Santa Cruz Transit District, using student fees to help subsidize a bus service every half hour from downtown to the campus. Cabrillo Community

College was also served, but the Transit District officers complained that the line suffered from insufficient use. And there was almost no service from the inland towns, where many students lived, to the campuses.

Cabrillo College organized a car pool, the drivers and riders being given stickers and cards of identification—which of course was no great proof against a determined murderer, although it sometimes helped. At UC they installed checkpoints and guards at both entrances to the big, heavily forested campus.

In the early months of 1973, all the terror in the surrounding countryside seemed to coalesce in Santa Cruz.

Cynthia was a large eighteen-year-old with straight blonde hair. In her family she was Cindy, and she had a younger sister named Candy.

The children grew up in San Francisco, but their mother remarried and moved to Marin County with her new husband. Candy went with them to attend high school.

Cindy, at seventeen, however, struck off for Santa Cruz to enroll in Cabrillo College, debating about whether she wanted to become a school teacher or a policewoman. In her freshman year the college had required her to live with a family because of her youth. Later she moved down near the beach with a girl friend. And again, just recently, she had gotten a babysitting job with a family downtown and was living in.

She shared her job in shifts with a friend named Pamela. And it was her custom to thumb a ride out to the college.

In the early evening of January 8, she was walking down Mission Avenue, the main thoroughfare that becomes a freeway that leads into another freeway that goes past Cabrillo College.

When she did not reach her class and did not return home that night, Pamela telephoned the police. Later she also alerted Cindy's family in Marin County.

News of Cindy's fate was not long in arriving. Less than twenty-four hours later, a California Highway Patrolman stopped beside a three-hundred-foot cliff on the coast south of

Carmel, doing a routine check for motorists who sometimes overshot the curve and for incautious photographers who occasionally took one backward step too many. He spotted what appeared to be neither of these, but a human arm sticking out of a plastic bag beside the road. Further search not only confirmed the finding but disclosed, strewn down the side of the cliff, strips of skin, portions of two legs, an arm, and a severed hand. A week later, a neatly severed human rib cage washed ashore back up the coast near Santa Cruz, a case of the crime returning to the scene of the murderer.

Since many other girls were missing from their California homes, certain identification by the pathologists was not completed until January 24. The remains were those of Cindy.

Scarcely had news of this latest killing reached the community than some men practicing sharpshooting in the mountains nearby came upon the decomposed body of the other missing Cabrillo student, Mary.

A tall, graceful girl from Buffalo, New York, she had arrived in Santa Cruz in the late sixties. At the time of her death she was studying at Cabrillo to become an English teacher. She left the campus one night and flagged a ride. The car that stopped for her was a blue station wagon.

Behind the wheel of the car was a slightly built, almost handsome young man of twenty-five named Herbert Mullin. A few years earlier Herbie had graduated from San Lorenzo Valley High School where he had been voted the Man Most Likely to Succeed. He had earned honors in both his scholastic work and athletics. For a time he studied science at Cabrillo College and then transferred to San Jose State College. Psychedelic drugs, religion, and Eastern thought began to occupy most of his time. A Catholic, he thought of entering the priesthood and applied to do so but was rejected by his chosen order. He became a heavy user of LSD—the best guess was one hundred times—and soon began to worry about his heavy reliance on drugs. Meditation, he hoped would help him to break free of them, and he worked on that.

His parents were religious, middle-class people who feared what they saw happening to their son and other young people.

Once Herbie, to shock his mother, announced that he had been "shacked up with a girl"—and her reaction was all he might have hoped for.

He drifted around, and predictably, was busted on a drug rap in 1968; but they gave him a break. He was placed on probation and hospitalized. Soon, however, he was out and back on narcotics. His frantic parents then had him committed to Mendocino State Hospital where one of the best drug treatment programs was being carried out. But this too resulted in failure. Shortly after Herbie got out he went back on drugs. For the next couple of years he was in and out of several mental hospitals in California and even one in Hawaii.

Once a patient was on the outside, no one bothered much about a follow-up. Recidivism was high. Meanwhile, Governor Ronald Reagan was closing down the state's mental hospitals, taking for him, the suspiciously liberal position that the "warehousing" of patients was inhumane and that they could be much better cared for in their "communities." It was true that new tranquilizers enabled many patients to be cared for by out-patient clinics. The catch was that most local governments were either unwilling or unable to assume the cost of expanding psychiatric wards and out-patient clinics to meet the booming demand, particularly in view of the fact that expected federal support had been impounded by the Nixon administration.

In the course of Mullin's erratic career in and out of mental hospitals, he began to develop some bizarre theories about the interrelation of human sacrifices and natural disasters. There was a lot of scare talk in the newspapers just then about an expected big San Francisco Earthquake. He heard voices—telling him to sacrifice a few lives and thus save California from sliding into the ocean. One generation would save the next.

Meaning to do his part, Mullin took a baseball bat and killed an old hobo with it.

And then, pursued by the voices that only he could hear, he proceeded to kill twelve other random victims—children, teenagers, men, women, and a priest. One of these was Mary, who enters this account because the manner of her dying seemed so much like the work of another mass murderer. At least, the sheriff's officers felt pretty sure there had to be two mass murderers working the area, although they still had no hard evidence.

The day that Mullin in his blue station wagon offered a ride to Mary, it happened that he had just finished reading Irving Stone's biography of Michelangelo (*The Agony and the Ecstasy*). Fresh and vivid in his mind was the account of the great sculptor's painstaking explorations of human anatomy. Also he had just received one of his telepathic must-kill "commands"— this one, he recalled, being from a local man whose picture was currently in the papers because he was running for county supervisor. Michelangelo and the supervisorial candidate fused in the fevered flame of Herbie Mullin's mind and there, in front of him and a little to the right, stood a pretty young woman with her thumb out. He slammed on the brakes.

As they drove along, and after she had vainly attempted light conversation, Mary turned to watch the passing scenery. He killed her easily and without a word, keeping his left hand on the steering wheel, plunging a knife into her chest and then into her back, piercing her heart.

He turned off the freeway and drove into the woods, pulled her body out of the car, and proceeded to dissect her torso, examining her heart, liver, and lungs. In the mad, mad mind of Herbert Mullin, he was just like Michelangelo.

When Edmund Kemper read about the discovery of Mary's body, he was outraged. Not only was some fool working his territory, using a technique that might easily be ascribed to him, but this new fellow was sloppy and careless. The way he left bodies around anywhere, you could tell he had never been trained in the use of dry leaves. If this kept up, it could blow the whole thing. And after his months of impeccable planning! If there was anything Kemper loathed, it was casual workmanship on a "hit."

It was not until a witness saw Mullin impulsively shoot a retired Santa Cruz fish dealer on a residential street and reported the car's description that he was captured by law enforcement officers. The lack of any apparent pattern in his killings had confused everyone. And even after Herb confessed to the thirteen deaths and explained his bizarre rationale, his motivations were not easily understood.

A jury found him guilty of taking ten lives (he was not tried for the other three), two of them being murder in the first degree, which required that he be adjudged sane. Superior Court Judge Charles Franich thanked the jurors. He advised them to go home and remove the trial from their minds.

"Don't even think about it," he said.

But Kenneth Springer, the foreman of the jury, found he could not so lightly dismiss the matter from his mind. When he got home that night, he wrote a letter to Governor Ronald Reagan. He sent copies of it to state representatives and to the state director of mental health.

"I hold the state executive and state legislative offices as responsible for these 10 lives as I do the defendant himself—none of this need ever have happened," Springer wrote.

"We had the awesome task of convicting one of our young valley residents of a crime that only an individual with a mental discrepancy could have committed.

"Five times prior to young Mr. Mullin's arrest he was entered into mental hospitals. Five times his illness was diagnosed.

"At least twice it was determined that his illness could cause danger to lives of human beings. Yet in January and February of this year he was free to take the lives of Santa Cruz County residents.

"According to testimony at his trial, Herb Mullin could and did respond favorably to treatment of his mental illness.

"Yet the laws of this state certainly prohibit officials from forcing continued treatment of his illness, and I have the impression that they, as a matter of fact, discourage continued treatment by state and county institutions.

"In recent years, mental hospitals all over this state have been closed down in an economy move by the Reagan administration.

"Where do you think these mental institution patients who were in these hospitals went after their release from institutions? Do you suppose they went to private, costly mental hospitals, or do you suppose they went to the ghettos of our large cities and to the remote hills of Santa Cruz County? . . ."

The following spring the California legislature overrode a governor's veto for the first time in three decades—and in so doing gave the legislature final authority to approve or reject any future closing of the remaining eleven state mental hospitals.

Simply keeping the "warehouses" open would be no solution to the problem, but it would give communities a breathing space in which to assess their abilities to provide local mental health care; and perhaps some federal moneys could be shaken loose in the meantime. It gave them a chance to put the horse in front of the cart again instead of vice versa, a maneuver for which the education of the taxpayer was all-important.

CHAPTER EIGHT

WALKING
TIME BOMB

ROSALIND, a bright, well-liked girl from an affluent coastal resort town, was just completing her studies in linguistics and psychology at UCSC. She lived downtown in an apartment on Mott Street which she shared with her friends Nancy, Virginia, Kathy, and Linn.

Sometimes Rosalind bicycled up the hill to her university classes.

On the evening of February 5—only days after Cindy's remains had been identified and Mary's body discovered—Rosalind left the apartment after dinner to attend a lecture on campus. Her roommate Nancy was under the impression that she planned to take a bus, since the day had been rainy. Rosalind was wearing her dark pea jacket when she left the house.

She did not return that evening, and her housemates quickly informed the police.

The same evening in another house in Santa Cruz, Alice, 21, a small Oriental girl weighing only about one hundred pounds, left for the University campus to do some research at the library and afterward attend a late class. She was from Southern California and in her senior year at UCSC.

Alice regularly hitchhiked to and from the campus. She shared living quarters with Julie, also Oriental, a former student who was working as a financial assistant on the campus. The two girls had grown up together in Los Angeles and remained the closest of friends. Alice, one of four sisters, was the daughter of an aerospace engineer.

She did not return from her evening class. Definitely, in Julie's opinion, Alice was not the sort of girl to leave town without telling anyone.

When Julie telephoned the police to report Alice's disappearance, she reported that she, like the missing Rosalind, had been wearing a dark pea jacket and that she carried a tote bag containing an I.D. card, a hairbrush, a UC health card, and an El Camino Library card, among other items. She also carried a photograph of a friend in Taiwan, where she had visited the previous summer.

Word of the two girls' vanishing swept quickly through the campus community. There was nothing to link them together since they had not known one another. On February 14, several squads of students began grimly combing the groves of redwoods, pines, and madrona that grow thickly over much of the campus, stumbling through underbrush along the canyons, searching for what they feared to find.

Adding confusion and spreading fear over a broader range, on the following day the body of a girl named Leslie, 21, was found in a remote part of the Stanford University campus in San Mateo county to the north. She had been strangled and left beneath an oak tree. Leslie's death, as it turned out, was unrelated to the Santa Cruz student murders.

In Marin County, a friend of the family of Cynthia or Cindy anonymously posted a reward for information leading to the apprehension of her killer.

The arrest of Herbert Mullin occurred on February 13. On February 15, in the Eden Canyon area of Alameda County, a good hour's drive to the north, the headless bodies of Rosalind and Alice were found lying about a dozen feet off the roadway. The hands of one body were missing. And later the heads of the two girls were found on the Coast Highway just south of Pacifica, a town below San Francisco. These remains were quickly identified. The second killer was growing careless or desperate, and he knew it.

Journalists and TV reporters were advancing so many lurid rumors about the nature of the murderer—that he (she?) was a member of a Devil cult, a homosexual, a transvestite, a lesbian, a medical student—that the judge imposed a gag order in Mullin's case. The killings to which he had confessed remained uncertain in the public mind, and in this vacuum speculation spread like a firestorm.

Although investigators did not think that Mullin was responsible for the killings of Anita, Mary Ann, Aiko, Cindy, Rosalind, and Alice, they were for a time unable to rule him out, and even had they done so, were forbidden to discuss the matter with journalists.

One of their keenest followers, Edmund Kemper, annoyed by the lack of information in the newspapers, took to dropping in more and more often at the Jury Room to drink beer where the off-duty officers hung out. Genial Big Ed was developing a growing capacity for malt liquors.

Up on the UC campus, enrollments had plummeted that spring, which was a new experience for a much sought after school. Few hitchhikers—only men—could now be seen. The illogical nature of the crimes made everyone feel vulnerable. There seemed little they could do beyond avoiding rides with strangers and locking doors at night. Not for the first time, an entire county learned what it was like to live in fear of random violence. And this was good business for a bad business: the sales of gun dealers were booming in Santa Cruz and nearby towns.

Kemper had the jitters like everyone else. One evening he drove down to the pier and threw an object as far out into deep water as he could, using his right arm. His left arm was still in a cast. He was still off his job with the Highway Division and was tired of being short of cash. Between trips here and there, he hung around his mother's house in Aptos. He flushed a tiny handmade ring down the toilet there. He drove out to the Santa Cruz dump to discard another object. Again, after dark, he drove down the coast a short distance and threw a few small items over the bank by the road. It was good that his mother was always at work in the daytime. As for the neighbors, they paid little attention to his comings and goings.

More and more often he was experiencing that old feeling of being a "walking time bomb." One Sunday, for example, he drove up to his mother's house to find Sergeant Michael Aluffi of the Santa Cruz County Sheriff's office pounding on the door. Christ!

"Can I help you?" Kemper called from the car. A young blonde girl sat beside him.

"Yeah," said Sergeant Aluffi. "Do you have a .44 magnum revolver with this serial number?"

"Yes, sir, I do," Kemper said, courteous and respectful as always.

It turned out, Aluffi said, that Kemper, in filling out the application, had stated he had never been in a prison or a mental institution or convicted of a crime.

Well, Kemper said, officially that was true since his juvenile record was sealed. And he had been only fifteen at the time of committing the crimes, so he felt entitled to eliminate any reference to that period of his past.

Sergeant Aluffi had been frustrated in trying to get information about Kemper's past through official channels.

"I'll have to take the gun in now," he said, "but I'll give you a receipt for it, of course. Then we'll check into the legal technicalities of the matter."

"It's upstairs," Kemper said, unfolding his enormous body from the car and starting toward the front door.

Sergeant Aluffi followed him. Suddenly Kemper hesitated and said, "Oh, I think it might be in my car trunk, not inside. Do you need it for some investigation?"

"No, this is just routine," Sgt. Aluffi replied.

He watched Kemper open the trunk, rummage around and produce the gun in a holster. Kemper handed it to Aluffi, who then began to write a receipt. The sergeant noticed nothing special about the trunk or its contents.

As he drove off, he glanced into the rearview mirror. Kemper and the girl were standing by the front door of the house.

The next day Kemper, thinking over the incident, was so tense he felt like climbing the walls. Why, they could even have had the house at 609A Ord Drive staked out. They could have been watching the little back garden and his comings and goings for weeks. Jesus! It had to stop somewhere. But also, it had to keep going for the simple reason that he could not stop.

Somehow the weeks passed. On the Friday before Easter (April 21) he drove up to the apartment he sometimes shared with a friend in Alameda, to see whether an expected compensation check had arrived. It had, but the forty dollars was nowhere near the amount he had expected. How did they think he could go back on his job, needing new Levis, underwear, and socks? For that matter, how did they think he could live? He was beginning to feel guilty about imposing on his buddy.

Kemper telephoned the state office to ask whether there had been an error in the payment sent him, but was told that he would receive no further money. His friend, who knew where Ed normally purchased his oversized work clothes, told him to relax. He went out and bought the items that were needed.

And Kemper went back to work for a few hours on the Highways job, but in the afternoon he again drove down to his mother's house in Aptos. It seemed to him that until he could work full time and earn some bread, it was wrong to go on sponging on his friend. He would have to return to living with his mother. He had a feeling, though, that it could not be for long. As he later phrased it, unconscious of the grisly pun, he had a strong suspicion that things were "coming to a head."

"I felt," he recalled, "that I was going to be caught pretty soon for the killing of these girls, or I was going to blow up and do something very open and get myself caught, and so I did not want my mother—. A long time ago, I had thought about what I was going to do in the event of being caught for the other crimes, and the only choices I saw were just accept it and go to jail, and let my mother carry the load and let the whole thing fall in her hands, like happened the last time with my grandparents, or I could take her life.

"Well, I guess that leaves me two choices. I could either do it in the open with her knowing what was happening, or I could do it when she didn't know what was happening."

Thus the murder of his mother began to take form, as in the "mercy killing" of his grandfather nine years earlier. Another good deed in a naughty world, to save her from the shame and heartbreak of knowing that her son was the murderer known in journalist's jargon as the "coed killer."

He remembered what an upheaval it had been for her to leave Montana and start over again in a place where his record was unknown. Sometimes he thought with pride of her achievements. As administrative assistant to the provost, as he was aware, she had to exercise tact and intelligence. He worried that she would feel remorse about having given him the "A" sticker for his car so that he could park on the campus.

He was thinking about the whole problem that Friday, of how things might best be resolved, "and I just started working myself up toward the act of killing her."

When he reached the house at 609A Ord Drive, his mother was still at work. He sat around the house and "made a few business phone calls unrelated to the problem."

Then he called his mother at the University to let her know that her wandering son was home again. Clarnell Strandberg (whose reaction to this news, whether of gladness or distress, will never be known) told him she would be attending a University function that evening, would dine out, and not return until late.

Edmund went out for a six-pack of beer. Returning to the house, he proceeded to drink beer and watch the television. As he waited for his mother to return, the evening hours passed slowly.

"I had wished to talk to her, really, before anything happened," he recalled. "It was my hope that she would go on good terms, and this was impossible because—well, I guess it would be good terms, because we hadn't really argued or anything when we talked on the phone."

Clarnell Strandberg was not home at midnight, so he retired. He awoke at two A.M. and checked her bedroom. Still she had not returned. Again Edmund slept. He awoke at four o'clock, and this time discovered that his mother was home in bed. She had been reading and had just turned out her small lamp when he entered the bedroom.

She asked, "What are you doing up?"

"Oh, nothing," he answered. "Just wanted to make sure you were home."

"I suppose you want to talk?" she asked.

Quite often their discussions had started late at night and had grown into rows. He recalled that this time her comment had not seemed to him "abusive." It was "just jive." "No," he said, hoping that nothing would happen to mar the harmony of the moment.

"Well," his mother said, "we'll talk in the morning."

"Fine," Edmund said. "Good night."

And with a feeling of relief, he returned to bed. But not to sleep.

CHAPTER NINE

EDMUND THE CONFESSOR

OFFICER ANDREW CRAIN was on desk duty at around eleven P.M. April 23 when the first call came from Pueblo, Colorado. The caller almost gave up trying to get through.

Imagine, if you will, Lee Harvey Oswald at a public telephone box in Dallas, trying to get through to the FBI in Washington, D.C. to confess that he had just shot President Kennedy and that he was the person everyone in Texas was looking for. Imagine him being told by the telephone operator that he needed another quarter, and by the switchboard operator that everyone was too busy to take his call because the president had just been assassinated; and finally, imagine Oswald getting through to a real flesh-and-blood FBI agent only to be cut off;

and then trying to call back and being told by the operator that he needed another dollar and fifteen cents, and by the switchboard operator that the agent he had just been talking with was now off duty, had gone out of town, and was not expected back until nine o'clock next Monday. Imagine Oswald sitting there in a public phone booth somewhere in Dallas, with a loaded submachine gun under his coat, and suddenly he becomes aware of the traffic roaring suggestively under a nearby freeway overpass . . .

Officer Andrew Crain picked up the telephone and said, "Officer Crain."

He heard the faint, faraway clinking of coins into a public telephone slot, and the operator's voice saying, "Go ahead, sir."

A man's voice, slurred as if the speaker might have been on drugs or drunk—but maybe it was just the bad connection—came on the line, saying, "Lieutenant Scherer is not there, is he? He's been looking for me."

"Who's this?" Crain asked.

"I'm not going to tell ya," said the caller. "This is no prank. He's looking for me, and I want to talk to him."

"I'll have to tell him who's calling."

Scherer was off duty. Crain thought, however, that he might get some information by stringing the guy along. Another garden variety of nut, probably, eager to confess to crimes he only wished he had the nerve to commit.

"Tell him," the caller said urgently, "it's about something he wants to straighten out. Will you do that for me, please? This is no bullshit, I got to talk to him right now. I'm going to call you back in half an hour, or an hour or so. Have him down there." He added something that Crain was unable to understand because of the bad connection.

Officer Crain leaned forward, straining to hear.

"Now what was that phrase that you stated?"

From far away the voice came back on the line. "Coeds. You know what I mean? Get him down there and I'll call back, and I want to talk to him."

"Is there a number where Lieutenant Scherer could call you back?"

"No," the caller said. "I'm not gonna play any games. I want to talk to him and I want him to do something."

"You can't leave me any kind of name?" asked Officer Crain.

"No!"

Crain said, "Unless I have something to go on, I can't wake up the lieutenant."

The voice, urgent and desperate, repeated, "Tell him it's not a prank. I'm not shitting you. Okay?"

"Do you have anthing to base it on?" asked Officer Crain, wishing to elicit some solid, airtight evidence of nonshitmanship if any existed—such as, maybe, a corpus delicti.

The caller then surprised Officer Crain by addressing him by his first name.

"Yeah, Andy. Ed Kemper. He's looking for me. I'm about two inches right now from doing a whole bunch of things. There's not really anything anybody can do about it unless I do something about it, you know? I want to talk to him."

"Okay," Crain said. "You're going to call back—when?"

"Oh, shit!" Kemper said. "What time is it there?"

Crain checked his wristwatch against the wall clock and said, "Eleven thirty-four right now."

"Yes," said the caller. "It's twelve thirty-four here, and that's part of the problem. I'll call back in—I hate to . . . How far from the station is he?"

"A half-a-mile, a mile."

"Okay," Kemper said.

The conversation lagged. Officer Crain decided to resynchronize their wristwatches, saying, "Eleven thirty-six now."

"Yeah," Kemper said. "It'll be roughly—I didn't want to tell you my name, really, Andy. This shit's got to stop quick."

"Okay, I'll notify him," Crain promised.

"Okay."

"Thank you," said Officer Crain.

When the telephone rang later it was one A.M., April 24, and

Police Officer Glenn S. Toriumi took the call. The long distance operator at Pueblo, Colorado was placing a collect call for Lieutenant Charles Scherer.

"Lieutenant Scherer is not here," said Officer Toriumi. "He will not be here until nine A.M. tomorrow morning. He's on a trip tonight."

A man's voice broke in urgently, "Can I talk to him?"

Officer Toriumi said, "I can't accept collect calls. If you wish to contact Lieutenant Scherer, like I stated, he will be in tomorrow morning at nine A.M."

The operator started to cut the connection, but the voice yelled, "Wait a minute! Wait a minute!"

Toriumi said, "Sir, I have an emergency line going," and hung up.

Edmund Kemper was never sure how many hours passed before he again tried to call. He thought perhaps it was six, but the Santa Cruz Police Department tape recording showed that it was five A.M. when the next call came in from Pueblo.

Again, a man was asking for Lieutenant Scherer. He found a new desk officer on duty. This one took the call, saying, "Officer Brown speaking. Lieutenant Scherer is not on duty at this time. What did you want to talk to him about last night?"

Kemper almost screamed through the static of another poor connection. "Coed killing!"

"What?"

"Coed killing!"

"The coed killing," mused Officer Brown.

"Killing, you know," Kemper shouted, still unsure if the officer understood.

"Yeah," said Officer Brown, and signaled his colleague, Officer Conner, to pick up an extension telephone.

"Where did you say you are?"

"Pueblo, Colorado. I want the police over here!"

"What's the address? Is it a home address?"

"No," Kemper said. "I'm saying—I lived in Aptos."

"Are you in Aptos now?"

"*No*," shouted Kemper. "I'm in *Colorado*."

"What's your name?"

"Ed Kemper."

"Where are you exactly, Ed?"

That was when Kemper said, almost incoherently, "I've been driving for three days steady. I have almost a nervous break-down right now—."

Officer Conner spoke up on the extension, "All right. Just tell me where you are and we'll have someone come and pick you up."

"Yeah," said Kemper. "That's what I want."

At Officer Conner's suggestion, he left the telephone booth, walked to the curb, and checked street signs not far from where his car was parked.

"I'll be at Twenty-first Street and Norwood Avenue in Pueblo," he said. "I'm driving a car I rented in Reno."

He described it. "It's a seventy-three Chevy, green—solid green—Impala."

At the request of Officer Brown, he again obligingly left the telephone booth to get the license number of the car.

"It's WBM-397."

"Okay, Ed, thanks," said Officer Conner.

"Yeah," Kemper replied. "Well, what I wanted to talk to Scherer about, there was eight people involved . . ."

Officer Brown: "There's eight people involved?"

"Not in what happened," Kemper said. "There's eight dead people."

Officer Conner spoke up. "Hey, Ed. While we're talking to you, we're going to have somebody come over."

"Yeah," said Edmund Kemper, "I wish to shit you would, really, 'cause I have over 200 rounds of ammo in the trunk and three guns. I don't even want to go near it."

Kemper later confided to investigators that he had chosen the long-distance-telephone approach because of his huge size, fearing that in any personal, unannounced confrontation, the police would have shot first and asked questions later. Physical violence terrified him. Although he did not personally know Lieutenant Scherer, he had seen him around Santa Cruz and knew that he was investigating the murders of the women students. Later, he told Scherer that he reminded him of his father, "the John Wayne figure in my life."

To keep Kemper on the telephone and talking, and maybe just possibly to get as much of a confession out of him as they could before having to apprise him of his rights, Officer Conner said, "Tell me about some of the killings—okay?"

"You want to know some of the details," Kemper said. "That's what I was going to tell Scherer, 'cause he'd know I wasn't talking crazy."

"All right. Just tell me."

"All right, the two UCSC girls. Okay?"

"Yeah."

"Okay, Rosalind_____. They didn't say anything about the physical evidence he found at the place, but she had some of her clothing on. She had a black pair of felt Navy pants, bell bottoms, with buttons; and panties. That was it, maybe a bra, but I can't remember. Okay?"

Officer Conner asked him about Cindy. But Kemper misunderstood and named another victim, Alice.

"No, Cindy."

"I'm telling you," Kemper said, repeating Cindy's last name, "there's six of them; and Saturday and Sunday there were two more, and it was my mother and a friend of hers."

"Where do they live?" asked Conner.

"Aptos."

"Have they been found yet?"

"No," Kemper said. "That's why I was blowing it last night, and those goddamn cops told me to call back this morning at nine o'clock."

Officer Conner asked him for the address in Aptos. This further hint of bureaucratic skepticism was too much. Kemper, fighting off hysteria in his telephone booth, ready to drop the phone and run for it, taking as much of the world's population with him as he could while the ammunition lasted, shouted, "What I'm *saying* is, I'm teetering between saying fuck you guys and run off and, you know, just blow it; or I'm trying to stop all this bullshit, man. Damn it! Just—"

"Okay, just calm down," said Officer Conner. "Okay?"

Where the hell, he wondered, were those Pueblo officers?

Kemper continued ranting. "I can't calm down. I'm not going to hang up or nothing, but I can't calm down. I'm wired up. Not on drugs or nothing. I've just been up three days. I'm kind of having a nervous breakdown, and it's not about giving myself up."

"Ed," Officer Conner said, "where does your mother live?"

He gave the address in Aptos, spelling the street name because Ord sounded like Ward, and saying it was a hard place to find because there were several houses all numbered 609, but this was six oh nine Able. And he suggested that they find Sergeant Mike Aluffi, who happened to know the house because he had been there recently.

"If you get him, if you have to get the sheriff anyway to go out . . . I can tell you how to get in and everything. Then you guys are gonna know I'm not bullshitting."

"Ord is the street?" asked Officer Conner.

Kemper repeated the address and Conner asked who was there.

Kemper said his mother and her friend were—or rather, he corrected, their bodies.

"My mother's name is Mrs. Clarnell Strandberg. She works at the University; so does her friend, or did. I blew it Saturday and killed my mother. And then Sunday this friend came over—no, Saturday night she came over—and I killed her. And then Sunday I just packed up all my guns and split."

"Okay!" said Officer Conner.

Kemper again became almost incoherent. For one thing, others were trying to grab the credit. "You see, what I'm saying is, there is a break somewhere. I can't tell you what's wrong with me, you know. But I had this big thought, you know, everybody thinks everything is cool, and then I pick up and split and say fuck it, I'm going to drive until I can't drive anymore, and then I'm going to just open up, you know? Driving all the way out here, I'm reading about some clown out in Idaho doing it, some guy out in L.A. doing it, Jesus Christ, you know! So now, last night I had a loose moment, I got pissed, I called up and tried to turn myself in. And they told me to call back this morning when Scherer was on duty!"

Officer Conner soothed him. "Yeah, they probably just tried to kiss you off, which they shouldn't do."

Kemper said he suspected that Officer Andy Crain had thought him "either drunk or fucking around."

He described his earlier efforts to get the message through, spicing his vocabulary as he often did with the lurid, sadomasochistic phraseology of comic books. (Later, in describing his crimes in monstrous detail, he would exchange the idiom of violence for that of the detached scientific observer, a carryover from his Atascadero learning. Thus he spoke formally of sexual intercourse instead of using a cruder word, even though both were technically inadequate for acts of necrophilia.)

"What's blowing my mind is, I thought you guys would be out here dragnetting me," he fumed.

By inference, what had been blowing Kemper's mind was that the cops might be dragnetting some clown in Idaho or Los Angeles. It was enough to drive a megicidal maniac to No-Doz, which was exactly what he had been dropping for the last three days.

In case the Santa Cruz officers were still in doubt, he added, "I was running."

"Give me a physical of what you look like," said Officer Conner.

This was more like it.

"I'm six-nine and I weigh two hundred and eighty."

"How old?"

"Twenty-four. And now that everything is up in the wind . . . Oh, shit! I'm usually a hell of a lot more in contact. I tried just to sleep, you know, last night. They said, call in the morning, and I laid there for six hours. I didn't even know it was six hours. I thought I was coming apart. I think I'm going out of my goddamn head and I've never done that before, you know, to where I don't know what's going on. And if that happens I don't know what's going to happen with all of these damn guns laying around."

He said he hoped Conner was getting some of this on paper, and Conner said he was writing it all down, that's why it was taking so long.

Kemper described the house in Aptos again, the only two-story *green* duplex in the cluster. He said he had locked it up when he left and taken all the keys with him. But if Deputy Sergeant Aluffi were to go there and enter the back yard near a tall gate, "There is this little tiny back yard, and there is a little plot of ground in back that is all choked up with weeds—."

Kemper was trying to convey to Officer Conner that there was a spare set of keys buried in the weeds right by the gate. This was not the only thing buried in the weed-choked little plot, but it seemed to be more than Officer Conner wanted to hear just then, for the officer interrupted to ask Kemper how he had killed his mother.

"With a hammer . . . I can give you all of the statements you want, I can cooperate and everything. But I *got* to get off the goddamn street."

Officer Conner was beginning to sweat too.

"All right," he said. "There is somebody on their way over there now. There should be."

What were they doing in Pueblo? Getting a search warrant to enter a public phone booth?

As the minutes ticked off, Kemper talked. He described the master bedroom with two closets, one a walk-in and the other a closet with big wooden sliding doors. His mother's body, he said, was in the walk-in closet, hidden by some clothing.

"Okay, where is the friend?" asked Conner.

"She is in the other closet . . . You got to move a big desk out of the way to get to the side she's on there, and her name is Sara Taylor Hallett. She goes by the name of Sally and she works at the University too, or did."

Still stalling for time, Conner asked him about the deaths of the two UCSC students, Rosalind and Alice. Kemper answered eagerly, telling him the general areas in which he had disposed of their beheaded corpses. He wanted to get it all out *now*—the waiting was coming to an end. But suddenly he broke off.

"The man's here. Whew! He's got a gun on me!"

"Let me talk to him," said Officer Conner.

CHAPTER TEN

"GAME PLAN" FOR MURDER

SERGEANT MICHAEL ALUFFI of the sheriff's department remembered Mrs. Strandberg's house.

"It is our policy," he recalled, "when receiving a dealer's record of the sale of a handgun, to check the person's name through the files to find out if they have been convicted of a felony." In Kemper's case, he had quickly learned of the 1970 parole by the California Youth Authority.

He had called the district attorney's office and then the CYA, but had been unable to get any information from the latter. "The authority that I talked to," he said, "stated that they had received a court order sealing his record."

Sergeant Aluffi's second visit to the green duplex on Ord

Drive, Aptos, was before dawn on the morning of April 24. By prearrangement he met another deputy there. Instead of going directly to the house, they woke up a few neighbors to ask whether anyone had seen Mrs. Strandberg lately. She had not been seen for a few days, and this was thought unusual.

With this information, the sergeant and his companion did not trouble to search for house keys among the weeds. They simply broke a rear window and entered the residence.

Sergeant Aluffi, when asked later if he had noticed anything on entering the house, testified, "A very strong aroma that is— you might say—concurrent with a person who has been deceased for an amount of time."

He and his companion, Sergeant Brook, had peered into closets. In the first closet, beneath an article of clothing, they saw blood and what appeared to be hair. And then they "withdrew from the scene" to notify other officers and to call for an identification technician. Asked what they had done until these specialists came, Sergeant Aluffi replied, "Secured the residence until their arrival."

In a matter of hours after the house had been examined, Sergeant Aluffi had talked with the Santa Cruz County District Attorney, conferred with law enforcement authorities in Pueblo, Colorado, and booked for a group to fly to that city. The party that left for Pueblo at two o'clock that afternoon consisted of enough authority figures to gratify the heart of even Edmund Kemper. Some of them would serve as his escort committee. In addition to Aluffi were the much-sought Lieutenant Charles Scherer, Richard Verbrugge of the district attorney's office, and the DA himself, a small, ambitious politician named Peter Chang, for whom mass murders represented a career stepping-stone as he hoped either to a superior court judgeship—for which he was then running and was subsequently defeated—or to the office of the attorney general. Chief Deputy District Attorney Christopher Cottle had been carrying the routine business of the office, had assisted in the prosecution of John Linley Frazier, and was currently handling the prosecution of mass murderer Herbert Mullin. The Kemper case, the "coed killings," looked like just what the doctor ordered for an ambitious politician. Headlines and free TV exposure. A sadistic mass murderer eager to confess to everything. So Chang went along to make sure it was all on tape, with no hitches and no loopholes.

Kemper was led out of his jail cell in Pueblo, wearing manacles. He greeted the delegation politely, both relieved and pleased to learn that his efforts would now receive the attention they merited. Physically, the gigantic prisoner looked pale and distraught, for he had scarcely slept for days.

The several men sat down in an office. A tape recorder was turned on and Kemper was informed "as per *Miranda*" of his full rights—to remain silent, to have a lawyer present, etc.

He waived everything—an extradition hearing in Colorado, and his rights as a citizen under suspicion for multiple slayings —and at once started pouring the events of the past eleven months into the tape recorder. What he said then and a few days later back in Santa Cruz was in part entered in the trial record five months later, as typewritten transcripts. Combined with what he admitted in court, it constituted what must surely stand as one of the most detailed, articulate, and chilling confessions of sadism, murder, mutilation, cannibalism, and necrophilia in the annals of crime.

Edmund Emil Kemper III was desperate to talk.

The long-awaited Lieutenant Scherer set the audio stage by showing his clear awareness that the tapes would become vital evidence in a trial for mass murder.

"Ed, we're down here to talk to you in regards to statements you made to the officers here at Pueblo, Colorado. . . . Are you fully aware of your constitutional rights, Ed?"

"Yes," Kemper said. "They've been explained to me twice today. I've signed both times."

But Lieutenant Scherer knew that one could not be too careful in such matters. "I understand that. But—."

"You have to give them to me anyway, right?" asked Edmund the Confessor.

"Yes." He repeated the statement of legal rights and asked Kemper if he understood them.

"Yes, sir," said the strung-out giant, adding that he very much wanted to discuss the matter which Lieutenant Scherer now alluded to as being "presently under investigation with us."

In recent months, Kemper had had ample time to think about what he might tell the officers if the chips were ever finally down, if he blew it and they dragnetted him. He had thought about how much should remain unsaid, and he had rehearsed it all many times. What he had not guessed was that the need to find catharsis in confession would become as overpowering as the original compulsion to commit the crimes that would need confessing to. Now the hunter was himself trapped, and not by the police or any other officers of the law.

With the tape recorder spools rotating smoothly, Lieutenant Scherer said he did not know what Kemper was about to tell them but advised him to put it all in his own words, starting with the first incident. "Tell us whatever details you choose," he invited. "Do this as though you were writing a letter to a friend in some distant place."

But Kemper, before getting into the story, wanted to have some legal technicalities straightened out, his concern betraying not an irrational state of mind as it might at first have seemed, but rather the extent to which he had considered all the potential legal angles. He told Scherer that he was worried about the problem of "county jurisdictions," since he had been operating in such a range of territory, and in the case of fifteen-year-old Aiko, with the possible charge of "abduction."

"I picked her up in Berkeley, and there was no problem on her part; she was *going* to San Francisco. She didn't know the area over there, so we went through San Francisco and were at Half Moon Bay before I told her what was going on as far as an abduction goes. But at that point, it was against her will, so technically it was in San Mateo County that I committed a kidnapping, and the actual murder happened in Santa Cruz County."

Kidnapping being a federal, capital offense, maybe the FBI should be sitting in on the confession. As if to compensate for the apparently inadequate attention received as a child, he would now insist on his full dues. Accounts Receivable. Now the authority figure had to listen, lending its surrogate ear for the father who had failed to do so.

Lieutenant Scherer replied that, "jurisdictionwise," he did not anticipate any problems. He stated that all this would be discussed with district attorneys of the various counties when the group returned to California. Insofar as the matter of abduction was concerned, he added that it "at this point is kind of a secondary situation."

Kemper, having demonstrated due concern for the legal niceties, then tested whether remorse might be well received.

"I went into some detail today on these cases, and I wish I hadn't now," he said, referring to his telephone conversation. "It's been bothering me more and more, just thinking about it, and then talking about it today with someone else. It just didn't really have an effect then. I told the officers that when I'm talking about something like that, from being in Atascadero for so long and talking about very serious things and very tender things, bothersome things, I get kind of calloused, you know, where I don't show emotion. I just talk, getting the thing out, and later on it hits me. I spent the whole afternoon in there trying to decide whether I was gonna climb the bars and jump off or hang myself . . . You know, I was really very seriously depressed about the whole damn thing, so I was hoping that— I suppose you're going to have to have something to go on prior to going back and really getting something laid out."

Lieutenant Scherer, not to be distracted by ephemera, asked for the record whether Kemper had been given any drugs or alcoholic beverages since he had been taken into custody at 7:30 that morning.

"No," Kemper said. "I have been treated very fairly."

And then the only witness to the last hours in the lives of Mary Ann, Anita, Aiko, Cynthia, Rosalind, Alice, Clarnell Strandberg, and Sara Hallett began to talk.

"Last May seventh at approximately 4 P.M.," Kemper said, I picked up two girls on Ashby Avenue, which is also Highway 13, in Berkeley, who were carrying a sign which said they wanted to go to Stanford.

"I asked them a few questions and determined to my satisfaction that they were not familiar with the area. Without pressing too hard, and doing a few loopy-loops around freeways and bypasses, I managed to think up some method for following through with this act with the least amount of jeopardy to me.

"What I did was, I stopped for gas in Alameda, where I was living."

At the station he went into the restroom, taking a map, and checked to make sure that Stanford University was to the south.

"So I took them the other way, out on 680, which would come in on the rural highway. I told them a story about how I was working for the Division of Highways. They were impressed with my radio transmitter, and they thought I was a secret agent or something. I kept telling them that I wasn't a policeman . . . and they'd give each other little looks. But I didn't really make much of an effort to deceive them because they were terribly naïve. Anything I said just went over fine."

Instead of going south, Kemper was heading east toward Livermore, a flat, hot town whose claim to fame was that it was the site of a University of California Radiation Research Laboratory. Kemper, however, was looking for a rural cul-de-sac, and he found one.

In the car under the seat he had a 9-mm. Browning automatic that he had borrowed from one of his earlier bosses. He pulled the gun, but had to force himself to do it, he told the investigators.

"I was scared, and kept telling myself I didn't really want to do it. But I was determined. I was very frustrated, because it was like a game to me. Up to that point, it always had been. It was a big adventure, a big thrill. But I never permitted myself . . . to follow through and take a chance on getting in serious trouble. . . . I mean avoid the possibility . . . of rape; but I had decided from my past stay at Atascadero and listening to a lot of stories, that what I thought was my past experience— it seemed to me a lot more efficient not to have someone, unless you're absolutely sure that they weren't going to go to anybody, and in this case, thinking back on it, I really honestly think I could have gotten away with doing exactly what I told them I was going to do, which was rape. I didn't say that word. But one of them asked me, 'What do you want?' and I pointed the gun. I just lifted it up between the two of them, and I told her, 'You know what I want.'

"The one girl, Mary Ann, assumed command over the two and over conversation, and immediately when I turned the gun up, I turned to her and spoke and ascertained from our conversations that she was not the talkative one, but the one who was more in a leadership position. The other girl was Anita, who was overpowered, despite the presentation of that weapon, without any threats."

It had upset Kemper that Mary Ann did not seem properly impressed by him and his gun, and she had even made the mistake of wisecracking a little. Very coolly and calmly, she had tried to dissuade him by using tactics which he recognized as those that would have controlled nine out of ten rapists. She sought to reason sympathetically with him, suggesting that he had problems she would like to talk with him about. But Edmund, having been exposed to such techniques in the hospital, said he had recognized them at once for what they were and was able to resist them. Even so, her huge, deep blue eyes would haunt him for months afterward. She awoke a feeling of tenderness in him that none of his other victims would.

"I was really quite struck by her personality and her looks," he said, "and there was just almost a reverence there."

Agitated and scared, Kemper was relieved when he found a deserted place to park the car. He told the girls that one of them must get into the trunk so that he would not have to keep an eye on her, while the other was to be hidden in the back seat. Then they would all go to Kemper's apartment in Alameda. But the girls did not seem to be appropriately respectful of his size, he said, even when they understood what he intended to do to them at his apartment.

When you had grown up in the sheltered places, it did not come easily to believe in the jungle. One had heard of such predators, but only other people met them.

Anita was quiet but Mary Ann continued her "very good efforts of communicating and discussing the thing, rather than just jumping hastily into action, before anything serious happened."

He said he explained to them "that if either one of them had gotten any funny ideas about communicating with anybody, or pulling the lights out in the back so I wouldn't have any signal for brakes, or something—I told them that that was going to be the end of both of them. . . .

"At this time, I had full intentions of killing both of them. I would have loved to have raped them. But not having any experience at all in this area, I'd had very limited exposure to the opposite sex and I guess the learning point—fifteen to twenty-one—I was locked up with all men, and there wasn't any opportunity to be with women or girls, and this is one of the big problems I had, and one of the biggest things that caused me to be so uptight.

"So even trying to communicate (with girls) before this happened, just casually, I felt like a big bumblebutt, and I think it's just like an over-aged teenager trying to fit in. They were both eighteen at the time, I think, and I was twenty-three, which isn't that much of a gap, but it was just like a million years.

"Anyway, I decided that Anita was more gullible and would be easier to control, so I told her that she was gonna go into the trunk. And she stepped right out of the car, and I had a pair of handcuffs I had purchased. I took the cuffs out and I reached for one of Mary Ann's arms and she grabbed it back. I picked the gun up like I was gonna hit her with it and told her not to do that again. I said, you know, 'I'm running the show here,' or some such cliche. So she allowed me to put my handcuffs on her arm, and I put the other one around the seat belt, behind the lock so it wouldn't come up, and left her back there.

"I took the other girl to the trunk. Just before she got in, she reiterated something Mary Ann said: 'Please don't do this,' or something like that. I said, 'What, are you gonna start in too?' "

Back in the car, he found that Mary Ann was not quickly following through on his instructions. "I almost stuck the gun up her nose to impress her that that was a real gun and that she kept getting me more uptight than I was. And then my lips started quivering, rather than her friend's, and I started losing control, and I told her that if she kept this up, that they were all gonna be in a whole lot of trouble. At this point, she cooperated. I handcuffed her behind her back and turned her over, and I tried to put a plastic bag over her head. I had this nifty idea about suffocating her. I was going to be really smart, and the windows were rolled up, and just normal conversation wouldn't carry—it was a fairly populated area. It was up on the hill. You couldn't hear voices or anything 'way off in the distance. So I didn't want anything carrying that would be conspicuous. . . . She was complaining that she couldn't breathe. I said I'd tear a hole in the bag, not intending to really, and I had a terrycloth bathrobe with a long rope tie. I put a loop in it and started pulling it down over what I thought was her neck. I pulled it tight. That's about where I blew it."

Kemper said he became overly tense and snapped the rope in two. It had caught her around the mouth anyway, and she complained. She also bit a hole in the plastic bag. Enraged, he reached into his pocket, pulled out his knife, and flipped the blade open. Blinded by the bag over her eyes and with her back to Kemper, she asked him what he was doing.

"I poised the blade over her back, trying to decide where her heart was, and struck and hit her in the middle of the back, and it stuck a little bit; and she said something like Ow! or Oh! and I pulled it back out.

"And I did it again and did the same damn thing, and I was getting mad now and I told her to shut up after the second time, and she said, I can't, and was moaning. She was struggling . . . but she couldn't move too much . . . Then I started thrusting hard and I was hitting, but apparently I wasn't hitting or the blade wasn't long enough, which wasn't conceivable to me because she wasn't that large a girl, rather small in fact, about five feet two inches and maybe 105 pounds. I struck in several places in both sides of the back and noticed as I went further down the back, that she was a little louder and more painful in her cries, but none got really loud. That always bothered me. I couldn't figure out why. It was almost like she didn't want to blow up and start screaming or something. She was maintaining control. But when I started doing this, then it got to be too much for her, she twisted around, and I hit her once in the side with the knife.

"She turned completely over to see what the hell I was doing, I guess, or to get her back away from me, and I stabbed her once in the stomach in the lower intestine. It didn't have any effect. There wasn't any blood or anything. There was absolutely no contact with improper areas. In fact, I think once I accidentally—this bothers me, too, personally—I brushed, I think with the back of my hand when I was handcuffing her, against one of her breasts, and it embarrassed me. I even said, whoops, I'm sorry, or something like that. She was pretty cognizant of what was going on, and it was getting pretty messy there in the back seat. She turned back over on her stomach, and I continued stabbing. I don't know how many times I stabbed her. I'm trying to think. I usually checked something like that—you might say, almost comparing notes—and in this case I didn't. I did with Anita, 'cause that really amazed me. With Mary Ann, I was really quite struck by her personality and her looks, and there was just almost a reverence there. I didn't even touch her, really too much, after that. That is, other than to get rid of physical evidence, such as clothing, and later the body.

"Anyway, she was across the back of the seat with her head down towards the door, towards the space between the front seat and back seat, and I don't think the bag was on. She had shaken it off. She was crying out a little louder, and I kept trying to shut her up, covering her mouth up, and she kept pulling away, and one time, she didn't, and like it was a cry, and I could have sworn it came out of her back. There were several holes in the lung area and bubbles and things coming out, and the sounds shook me up, and I backed off; at that point, she turned her head to the back of the seat and she called her friend's name, her first name. It was slow and it was not loud. That was the last thing that she said. She wasn't passing out at that point. I don't think at that point that the full impact of what had happened had really hit her. I think she was pretty well in shock or something.

"I felt I was getting nowhere, not that I wasn't getting any kicks out of stabbing her, but hoped that one would do it. When it got quite messy like that, I reached around and grabbed her by the chin and pulled her head back and slashed her throat. I made a very definite effort at it, and it was extremely deep on both sides. She lost consciousness immediately, and there were no more vocal sounds anyway."

At that point, Kemper got up in a daze or shock, he said, and headed to the back of the car. "I knew I had to do it to the other girl right then, because she had heard all the struggle and she must have known something very serious was going on."

He concealed his hands as he raised the trunk lid because of the blood on them. Anita said, "What's happening with Mary Ann?" Kemper said, "Well, she was getting smart with me."

"And I pulled my hands down kind of unconsciously, and she noticed how bloody they were and she panicked. Her lip was really quivering, and she was really scared. I was scared."

He told her that he thought he had broken Mary Ann's nose and that she should help her. Anita, in her new, heavy coveralls, started to get out. While Kemper was talking to her, he picked up another knife from the trunk, with a very large blade. "It was called the Original Buffalo Skinner or something," and it had been "very expensive, about eight or nine dollars."

He turned to Anita with the Original Buffalo Skinner and

stabbed her hard as she got out of the trunk, but the knife vexingly failed even to penetrate her garments.

Anita saw what was happening. As Kemper stabbed at her again and again, she threw herself back into the trunk, saying "Oh, God, God." She began fighting back. He tried to slash her throat but in the process stabbed his own hand, a fact he did not realize for all of an hour. He did not however fail to take account of the fact that when he went to the office of Dr. Donald G. Miller in Aptos for treatment, the wound required three stitches.

As Anita tried to cover her throat with her hands, he stabbed through her fingers. She was, as he told the investigators, "putting up a hell of a fight." He then tried to stab her heart. "I was thrusting and the knife was going very deep, and it amazed me that she was stabbed three times and she was still going at it. I tried stabbing her in the front again, or towards the throat area, and she was making quite a bit of noise and was trying to fight me off, and I stabbed her in the forearms. One was so bad you could see both bones, and she saw it, when I hit, I didn't think it really hurt so much, as it was the shock of everything happening so fast. She looked at it, and I could see the expression on her face of shock."

The details of butchery that caused veteran law enforcement officers to shudder, Kemper had gone over again and again in private and only partly in preparation for just this penultimate, glorious, megicidal catharsis. Today the officers and the tape recorder; tomorrow there would be judge, jury, press corps, bailiff, spectators, young girls seeking his autograph. Sane, SANE, SANE! They would have to find him sane of course, for the public feared not to.

And if by chance a reporter forgot or felt ashamed to ask him what it felt like to rape a dead and mutilated body or to perform the ultimate obscenity of the living against the dead, he himself would raise the question, relishing the interviewer's horror, for only in this way, once his deeds ran their course, as they had now, could he continue to exact his Accounts Receivable. The exquisite remembrance. If there *were* any justice in the world, which of course there was not, they would take from him neither his freedom nor his life. What they would take would be his sadist's memory.

He continued stabbing young Anita, trying to jab her left eye, as he told the assembled lawmen.

"I hate to get into such detail on that," Kemper apologized, "but my memory tends to be rather meticulous."

Finally, Anita began screaming, very loudly and piercingly. Her murderer was scared, he said, and unsure of what to do. He had heard voices in the distance. Therefore he renewed his attack with greater fury. The stab with which he hoped to penetrate her eye socket failed, but he knocked her glasses off.

"She reacted to each one of these things with a completely different thing," Kemper noted. "Where the other girl was just one continuous motion, this girl was actually fighting me, almost succeeding. But she really didn't have a chance."

He said that she started dying. She slowed down and became semiconscious or delirious. She was moaning and waving her arms around, fending off an imaginary assault that was no longer there. Every motion of the victim fascinated him, registering itself on his mind. Finally, he threw the knife into the trunk of the car and shut the lid. He noticed that she had torn off his wristwatch and that it was stained with blood.

He checked the back seat of the car and found Mary Ann slumped there, dead. He pushed her body down on the floor and covered it with an old leather jacket. Then he began to panic. He could not remember where he had thrown his gun. He thought he might have thrown the car keys into the trunk too, but found them in his back pocket.

"I said, 'Oh, Jesus, that's just what I need, and a bunch of people are gonna be charging up here any second.' And I ran around the car looking for anything that might have fallen out." And by the passenger side of the car he found Mary Ann's wallet. He thought at first she might have thrown it out deliberately, but later, finding blood on it, decided it had occurred accidentally after he began to attack her. Kemper threw the wallet back into the car.

"I jumped in the car," he recalled, "and was sweating very heavily and there was blood splattered here and there and on my hands, which I had to keep concealed. But I drove out of the area. Very close by, right down on the main road, were two couples looking at property. They looked rather disgruntled as I went by. I tried to look nonchalant."

About a month later he returned, as he always did, to the site. In fact for almost a year Kemper retoured the scenes of murders and the places where he had disposed of body fragments, in the manner of some fastidious and overly concerned cemetery caretaker. There were several reasons for this: an effort to recapture the excitement and horror of the deed, and perhaps, subconsciously, the wish to be caught and punished; but also his concern for the success of his game plan, his desire for perfection, and the needs of his insatiable curiosity. If he were to continue paying back society with hatred, he must re-assure himself that society and specifically the law were not onto his game. The possibility of a stake-out both scared and attracted him. Sometimes when he returned to a burial site, he inflicted an additional obscenity upon the dead.

And the thing that always impressed him was the almost one-hundred-percent safety of being a murderer in the land of the self-absorbed and fearful. Many times people saw things that hinted of his crimes and deliberately looked away. In the eyes of the law, he resembled Mr. Clean and Mr. Square. They never looked twice. And Kemper, to prolong the game, learned another role. He became Mr. Careful.

When he returned to this place of murder about a month later on his motorcycle, he found that a steel gate had been erected at the entrance on the main road. He speculated that the property owners "had been very much aware something bad had happened. They apparently thought a rape . . ."

The officers hearing his confession asked what happened after he had killed the two girls and driven out of the dead-end road.

It was then about six P.M. With his victims in the car, he drove to his Alameda apartment but was disconcerted to find a number of people down in the garage. Instead of going in, he pulled away again and parked nearby. He went upstairs, washed the blood off his hands, and bandaged the cut on his hand. Returning to the car and now killing only time, he drove around for a while. He stopped at a store and made some purchases. That was when he realized that he had not even checked on whether Anita, in the trunk, was actually dead.

Returning to his apartment garage, he was relieved to find it deserted. He opened the trunk of the car. The girl was dead. But he could not get over it.

"What surprised me was how many blows she took. They were all heavy blows. I didn't think I could have taken one of them. For them being such small females, both of them about the same size and build, the knife had to go well over halfway through her chest from side to side, and they were direct. It was shocking to me. But anyway, she was in a rather peaceful position, with one arm across her chest. That is also where the bloodstains on the jumpsuit came from. It was under her."

He told the officers about washing his jumpsuit—and washing it—to get rid of massive bloodstains. But they would not go away and remained in the cloth, a faint brownish-red.

"My intention all along," he said candidly, "was to get rid of any physical evidence that might make someone suspicious, and like I said to the officers today, when I discussed this, the whole series of things was very sick, I realize that better than anybody. The thing that hits me is that when I'm lucid and thinking normally and rationally, it's very painful at that point. But I had set up certain rules. What these were, were fantasies come to life. I decided I was tired of hiding in my little fantasy world while the rest of the world was trampling upon my head with their just living their normal lives. So I decided on this rebellion . . . like conquests or something like this, physical sights, my fantasies were usually around women. Rather than like having an orgasm with a dead woman or something; that was my fantasy, but it would be more along the lines of a not-so-forceful rape, or I would be in command and she would not be that unwilling; but I imagine everybody likes to have dreams like that. Mine did get a little bit more lurid than that."

What had he done next?

He decided to carry Mary Ann up to his apartment and proceeded to wrap the blanket around her body. He had not realized, however, that the murder knife was tucked in a fold of the blanket. It clattered to the concrete floor as he started to carry her out of the garage, and then he heard a car turning into the garage. Kemper rushed back to his own car with his burden and crouched behind it in the darkness. As for the bloodstained knife, it lay where it had fallen at the doorway. He could see the driver of the car. One of his neighbors in the building, a small Filipino Navy steward. The man was just returning from a Sunday afternoon musical affair. Quick action was needed to prevent his picking up the murder weapon.

Kemper emerged from hiding and walked slowly, coolly toward the doorway. The small man had seen the knife. He spun quickly around. There was fear in his face and in his voice.

"Is that yours?" he asked.

"Yes," Kemper said. As he retrieved the knife, the man fled upstairs.

Kemper followed him and stood for a minute or two outside his apartment door, listening. There were no sounds from within of a telephone call or conversation, so he returned to the garage.

This time he carried Mary Ann's body to his apartment, disrobed her, and proceeded to dissect her. He also decapitated Anita.

Later he checked through the girls' belongings, found that they had exactly $5.28 between them and took the money. Then he found an extra three dollars tucked into the lining of a sleeping bag, which he said he thought rather sneaky and clever. He was extremely interested in examining the girls' identification cards and noting their home addresses, particularly Mary Ann's. He planned to check that out later.

Sergeant Aluffi asked if he had any of their property left.

Kemper said no. He had kept this little handmade ring of Cindy's for a time on his desk, but had recently flushed it down the toilet. That was shortly after Aluffi questioned him about the gun.

In one of the girls' knapsacks he found the complicated German camera, and deciding that he would be unable to operate it without getting instructions, he took a hatchet-hammer and bashed it to pieces. While it might, he thought, have brought as much as seventy-five dollars in a pawn shop, it would also be exactly the sort of thing that an investigator might try to trace. He disposed of the pieces of the camera in various trash bags, which became his usual method later in getting rid of incriminating evidence.

The thing about cameras was that he already had this Polaroid, which was easy to use and quickly rewarding. The pictures that he took and kept for secret viewing were soon dog-eared, capturing as they did the fantasies after they had been acted out; and by poring over them he was able to reexperience the entire process, which was almost as good as a fresh kill.

Kemper told the investigators that he cut off the girls' heads to delay identification of their bodies should they be found, but like most of his motivations this was only partially true. The act of beheading, like severing hands, filled a subconscious need which he, least of all, understood. He said that he worried too about identification through dental records; and he described his problems in finding suitable burial places for such remains.

He drove into the rugged Loma Prieta area of the Santa Cruz mountains and began to bury a plastic bag. It was white and stained with blood. A young couple wandered nearby and their dog began to bark at Kemper. The white bag was the one he had tried to suffocate Mary Ann with, and he felt sure they had seen it.

"The couple suddenly went quiet," he said. "They called their dog, got into their car, and took off."

This scared him. Either they were getting the hell out of there, not wishing to become involved, or they had gone to notify the police. Working quickly, he disguised the burial site with great care and felt thankful to the Boy Scouts of America for their teachings.

When he later returned to this site, he was pleased to find that it had not sunken in at all. This was an area where young people stopped to drink beer "and things," and he had been afraid someone might start poking around.

The white plastic bag contained Mary Ann's body. The heads he kept for a time. Then he pitched them down a steep slope into a ravine. And in August, hikers found that of Mary Ann, who was indeed identified by her dental charts. Later he led investigators to the grave where he had buried her.

"Sometimes, afterward," he testified in court, "I visited there . . . to be near her . . . because I loved her and wanted her."

The remains of Anita were never found, but a corpus delicti was established based upon her disappearance with Mary Ann, on her habits as a girl who would not voluntarily have vanished, and on Kemper's confession.

When Kemper said that he had buried Mary Ann's head on May 8 but that it was not until August 15 that it was found, Sergeant Aluffi asked him how he could be so definite about dates. He said that he remembered all of them very well.

"I can't get it out of my mind. It got heavier and heavier, and harder and harder, and I drank more and more, and I came close to blowing it every time I'd drink too much. I don't mean doing something crazy, but almost *giving* myself away. The farther along I went, you'll have to agree, the sloppier I got and the more careless I got, both in picking girls up, taking chances, and not following my set rules, and also in the disposal of evidence."

He had considered his first two murders (as an adult) "very effective" because nothing was found for a long time. This meant the girls would remain on a missing persons list, he thought (not knowing their parents had been denied even this minimal help for a long time), rather than on a homicide list, which Kemper said would have meant immediate investigation.

And if he knew of a possible witness in the form of a certain highway patrolman who had passed him when the girls were in his car on Highway 680. The patrolman had looked them over very closely because it was obvious that they were hitch-hikers and that Kemper was not with them, "and he just eye-balled the hell out of me as he went by, and if they had been discovered dead the next day, I'm sure he would have remembered enough about the car or me to give me a lot of trouble."

The lives of six women might then have been saved.

At one point early in his Pueblo recital, Sergeant Aluffi asked him to hold up because the tape had gotten "all messed up." And Kemper commented, "Oh, Jeez, wouldn't this make a good horror story on tape?"

Before that day's taping ended, Kemper had described the two girls' physical appearances, clothing, and effects in ex-quisite detail and had enlarged on his attraction to Mary Ann, whose very large blue eyes had so deeply affected him. Her European address book and her Bear Mountain Ski Patrol card further convinced him that she was a daughter of the affluent class that he most envied. He told of driving hundreds of miles to view the family home in a "country-club district" to verify his suspicions. Yet the real reason he was drawn to visit the place where she had grown up went deeper, and he could only try to explain it.

A horrified courtroom later heard his taped voice saying, "I don't really want to go into such detail tonight on all of them, 'cause I'm probably just gonna go back and beat my head on the wall. But that particular one, I would say, the whole ex-perience is the most inlaid in my mind; you might say it had a very strong influence on the fact that I did continue doing these things.

"I think personally, down deep, that I continued to do these things to try and get *that* out of my mind, to cover it up, other young ladies, trying to get *them* out. I think possibly because of the way they died, and I had been very struck by Mary Ann and I had never really taken a chance on getting to know her at all, forcibly, I mean, getting to know her, not so much by rape, but even talking with her, and then I've had a lot of dreams about that and been very depressed about it.

"Like from there on out, it was easy. There was very little remorse for the young ladies, except the last two—that really blew me out, the reaction that the campus had."

At that point in the replay Judge Brauer interrupted to order a ten-minute recess.

CHAPTER ELEVEN

TRIUMPH OF THE HUNTER

HE WAS CRUISING down University Avenue in Berkeley around seven o'clock in the evening when he spotted "this Oriental girl" holding up a piece of paper with the letters *SF* printed in red marking pen. He had actually gone past before he spotted her. She and the scene looked right. He circled around the block, returned, and pulled up at the curb beside Aiko.

"There was absolutely no problem," he recalled. "Apparently she was not an accomplished hitchhiker."

Considering that Aiko was not even an accomplished automobile rider, it was obvious that Edmund Kemper's powers of observation were remarkably acute.

He found her completely trusting. "I didn't come across any of the normal problems I had with girls and their curiosity as to where I was going, what I was doing . . ."

Aiko knew the name of the off-ramp she should take into San Francisco to reach the dance studio and told him. Kemper's plan, however, was to go south toward San Jose, trying to get as close as possible to the cut-off to Coast Highway 1 before having to inform her that she was being abducted. So they did a number of loops around the on- and off-ramps to San Francisco.

"After blowing her off-ramp and making it sound like an accident," he recounted to officers, "I said, 'Whoops,' and she said, 'Whoops.' I think it was slightly cutting."

He whipped around more ramps in confusing succession. At one point, he chose what he thought was the ramp which he seriously believed she wanted him to take to reach her destination, but it turned out that he had made an honest error—one of very few in his career of crime. When he next emerged on the freeway, they were quite near the Coast Highway turn-off leading toward Santa Cruz, and the moment that might have saved the girl's life was gone. They were quite a long distance down the coast and nearing the resort area of Half Moon Bay before Aiko appeared to realize what was happening.

She turned to him, protesting that she would be late for her class. Kemper then told her that she would not be going to San Francisco. At once she started pleading with him not to kill her. He shook her with his right hand, telling her to "knock it off." While knowing that he meant to kill her, he assured her that she would not be harmed.

At first he had found her a very easy person to talk with, "quite intelligent, and she grasped the situation right away. When I told her, 'I'm afraid you're not gonna make that ballet class tonight . . .' immediately she took it as permanent and panicked and said, 'please don't kill me; you know, that type of thing, and was shrieking sort of. I pulled out this great .357 magnum six-inch Trooper that I borrowed from (a friend) who works where I worked at the Division of Highways . . . him not knowing what I was using it for."

He poked the gun into the slightly built adolescent's ribs. "Do you know what this is?"

But he managed to persuade her that it was himself he was planning to kill. He said he was depressed, and that he merely wanted to talk to her at his mother's house. The neighbors, however, would be suspicious if they saw her sitting in his car, and he therefore wanted her to get into the trunk. Aiko suggested instead that she sit in the back seat. She was whimpering.

Kemper jabbed her again with the gun, saying, "Now behave. I don't want to hurt you or anyone else. But if you try to signal a policeman or anyone else, I'll have to kill him and you. You wouldn't want to be responsible for the death of a man who probably has a family and kids, would you?"

In the Santa Cruz region, he drove into the mountains on Bonny Doon Road, turned off on Smith Grade Road, and drove until the car was screened by trees from approaching traffic. He remembered a fence there, with the sign, "Protected by Globe Agency," and if Kemper had noticed it at the time, he would not have parked in such a spot. But the detectives for Globe, or the electronic warning system if any, did not come to the rescue of Aiko that night.

He told the frightened girl that before taking her to his mother's house he would have to tape her mouth and tie her up, a story that must have struck her as most unconvincing.

Kemper produced a roll of medical tape, tore off a strip, and told her to assist him in placing it across her mouth. She did so and even, at his command, tested to make sure that her lips were sealed.

It seemed to him that she was not really alarmed until he lowered his huge body onto hers, stuffed his thumb and index finger into her nostrils, and began to suffocate her. Her arms were still free. At this point, Aiko went berserk and began to fight for her life. She struggled violently, tried to grab his testicles, and at first succeeded. (Elsewhere in his confessions, he told officers that he "felt bad" about her "particular case," because she had been totally cooperative and naïve in trusting him up to that point.)

For a tiny girl she fought like a tiger. Kemper was trying to pull a cord around her wrists while Aiko, suffocating, began kicking at the window. He kept his grip on her nostrils and the tape on her mouth through it all. When she stopped struggling, he released her nostrils. She was unconscious but breathing slightly. He remembered very clearly how he opened one of her eyes as a doctor might, to check for movement. But then her other eye opened and she again began struggling.

"For a moment she just looked at me, and I guess she became conscious enough, to where she remembered what was happening, and went back into the extreme panic she had been in, and the whole process started over again, for just about the same amount of time, identical to the other forty-five seconds. Every move—I mean, still grabbing at my testicles and still grabbing at my body."

This time he held her nose until all breathing stopped. She was into great, deep gasps with her lungs, he said, her back was arching, and she was unconscious. The breaths came fewer and farther between. Kemper said he still kept his fingers over her nose.

While she still breathed slightly but was unconscious, he carried her out of the car, thrust her body on the ground on her back, pulled down her pants "violently," forced sexual intercourse on her, "and I achieved orgasm—I guess it was only fifteen to twenty seconds. It was very quick. At that time I noticed her hair falling over her face and nose. She was still breathing, starting to breathe again. I took the muffler that she had around her neck still and just wrapped it very tight and tied a knot in it and . . . I even choked her around the throat for a moment, but by that time I was convinced that she was dead. Picked her up by the shoulders, and she wasn't a heavy girl. I think she told me she weighed 104½ pounds."

The fractions of pounds and of years counted to such a small, brief life.

He wrapped the blue blanket that had been in the trunk around her body and placed it in the trunk. The cord he had tried to tie her wrists with he had salvaged from Mary Ann's and Anita's camping gear. It was braided nylon "that was probably I'd say between a sixteenth of an inch and an eighth of an inch thick, and round, and it was burnt on the ends to keep it from unraveling." And this very useful material he returned to the trunk too.

Next, he checked the temperature of the girl's body and found it becoming cold. He drove back toward town, stopping at a little bar near Bonny Doon Road for a couple of beers.

"Also, to check up to see how apparent my—whatever it was, grief, excitement, exultation, anxiety—whatever, was showing. I wanted to test on these people in the bar and correct it before I went any further. Besides, I was hot, tired, and thirsty."

He checked the trunk before going in. In the bar he drank two or three beers, washed his hands in the washroom, and left, feeling that he had passed muster. Outside again, he reopened the trunk and glanced in, "to be satisfied that she was dead."

He added, "I suppose as I was standing there looking, I was doing one of those triumphant things, too, admiring my work and admiring her beauty, and I might say, admiring my catch like a fisherman. I closed the lid, got back into the car, drove to Santa Cruz, out to Aptos, where I stopped at my mother's home . . . and went inside the house.

"I talked to my mother for approximately half an hour about nonessential things, just passing the time, telling her why I was down from the Bay Area, which was a lie, a fabrication, testing on her whether or not anything would show on my face or my mannerism or speech as to what I was doing and why, and it didn't. She absolutely took no alarm or asked any undue questions.

"I left her home and by then it was probably nine-thirty at night."

In Berkeley it would be another two hours before Aiko's mother became alarmed and called the dance studio.

When Kemper left his mother's house, he was still feeling his power and could not resist opening the trunk, "again admiring my catch. Knowing already she was dead, feeling her body to see which parts were still warm, partially out of curiosity; and I wrapped her body up very firmly in the blanket because there was a big hole in the back that would catch dust and road dirt and things in it. The trunk was a very dirty area. I started driving again."

This time Kemper's travels took him back to the apartment in Alameda. He arrived at around eleven o'clock, carried Aiko's body upstairs, and placed it on the bed.

In minute detail he described her few possessions, the contents of her purse, her school equipment. The woolen muffler was solid white, crocheted, and it looked to him as if she or a member of her family might have made it. She had also a little pen pouch "that was very crudely made by crocheting, and she had crochet materials and tools in her bag. I gathered it was an article she had made herself."

He examined her pencils and pens and a large typewriter eraser. One of the pencils was blue, fairly new, and apparently, he recalled, had not been used much but just kept because it had her name on it. "She had scraped the enamel away, down to the bare wood, for about half an inch or three-quarters of an inch, and had written her name in blue with a ballpoint pen, and had etched it, actually, into the wood, her full name. . . . In fact, she had a little flower pattern in it. It was a little stem with four little dots around it."

He told about the impressions he had formed of the girl while talking with her.

"This was something I usually tried—to talk to the girls about, and gently probe about, different things; to find out their life-style, their living conditions, whatever. She was very free and prolific in her speech, and I believed from her speech that she came from a home of meager means, that her parents had either divorced or her father had left her at an early age, and she and her mother apparently were living alone, and possibly someone else. That wasn't quite cleared up.

"And there was no family car. The only transportation that she had was a bus to and from where she would go. I got no indication at all that she was from a family of any means. Her clothing was rather plain and she apparently had taken pains to dress herself—well, I don't know how to say it exactly, but as clean-cut as possible. Rather than just wear her hair long, she apparently had gone to some effort to look a little better dressed than she actually was."

At first glance he had thought her a full Oriental. "I only saw bits of her hair from under the hat, and it appeared to be black. But when she pulled her cap off and her hair fell out, and also on the back seat when I was choking her, I noticed that it was a dark brown and almost had some auburn highlights to it, but it was not black. It was definitely brown and not black, and that surprised me ..."

He remembered something else among her possessions—"a little leather coin purse with a little thong-type drawstring on it, and I think, little blue beads on it, with a few coins in it and also a house key. It was a nice new shiny house key that looked like it got very little use. This I later threw away. She had a great roll of yarn for crocheting, and she had a crocheting needle and a couple of knitting needles, or I should say, crocheting hooks. She also had several papers, corrected math papers from some school, with her name on them and the dates."

Her belongings he disposed of mostly in various trash cans.

While spilling it for the machine, Kemper broke off suddenly with an aside to Sergeant Aluffi, "There goes *my* law suit out the window." He said that his own attorney, who had been handling a $100,000 action for him, probably would no longer care to represent him.

This was in connection with the motorcycle accident in which he had broken his left arm, and what reminded him of it was the difficulty encountered when he carried Aiko's body upstairs to his apartment. He felt he was quite fortunate in getting her up there without anybody seeing him, but getting her back down again presented more difficulty—and it was because of this, he claimed, that he decided to dissect the body.

Her head and hands he took to a ravine behind a eligious camp above Boulder Creek in the Santa Cruz Mountains. The ground was hard and he dug a very shallow grave.

As in all his burials, he returned to check it later and on one occasion disposed of two more bodies nearby.

He spoke further of the exultation he had felt in slaying female victims.

"I just wanted the exultation over the party. In other words, winning over death. They were dead and I was alive. That was the victory in my case." But the act of decapitation he found sexually exciting.

"I remember . . . there was actually a sexual thrill . . . It was kind of an exalted, triumphant-type thing, like taking the head of a deer or an elk or something would be to a hunter. I was the hunter and they were the victims."

Yet sometimes it seemed to him (or seemed worthwhile asserting, in any event) that death was never a factor that entered into his killings. For he switched on the witness stand, after pleading insanity, claiming it was like when he had killed the cat as a child, "to make it mine." Thus he had killed the young women because, "Alive, they were distant, not sharing with me. I was trying to establish a relationship, and there was no relationship. . . . When they were being killed, there wasn't anything going on in my mind except that they were going to be mine. . . . That was the only way they could be mine."

Describing where he had buried Aiko's remains, he mentioned that it was "amazingly close to where the girl from Cabrillo was found up there, stabbed."

He was referring to Mullin's victim, Mary, whose death had so worried and angered Kemper. Pure coincidence, that was.

And Kemper could not help bragging that, to the very day of his confession, the Berkeley police still listed Aiko as only a missing person. "There was absolutely nothing ever turned up."

He described driving to Fresno for the psychiatric examinations and court hearing two days after murdering Aiko, boasting about the "positives" from the doctors.

But he could not help feeling somewhat let down when he

learned that the girl whose head was then in the trunk of his car was not of the moneyed class whose death would serve as a punishment of society for its treatment of him. Still, he was surprised to hear that she came from an "aristocratic type of family."

On May 17 the following year, the Santa Cruz County Grand Jury was convened to hear pathologist Hans Dibbern testify that he had examined body parts "known in the coroner's record as Aiko." These few bones had been little enough to go on, but judging from their size and delicate contours, they appeared to come from a female person about the age of fifteen years and four months. Dr. Dibbern said that such a person had been identified "recordwise as Aiko."

CHAPTER TWELVE

ANOTHER TROPHY

AT FIRST KEMPER'S time bomb operated at intervals of every four months. That space elapsed between his murders of Mary Ann and Anita, and the killing of Aiko. And then after a similar period of time, he discovered that the day was January 8, 1973, and he knew he needed to buy a gun and use it at once.

He drove to the Valley Shop in Watsonville, parked the banana-colored Galaxie hardtop at the curb, and strode in. Big Ed, the man they called "Forklift" on the highways job, clean, genial, and courteous, was just then having a hard time concealing his surging excitement. He filled out the permit—for a different gun from the one that Sergeant Aluffi was later to check on.

This gun was a .22 Rugers automatic pistol, ". . . uh, with a six-inch barrel; and that night I killed her . . . not so much to celebrate, but I had been eagerly awaiting that gun. I went bananas after I got that .22."

He had bitten his fingernails, Kemper told the stupefied interviewers, wondering why an officer had not raced out to the house to arrest him for purchasing the handgun—which perhaps was why he lost absolutely no time in staging his next safari for female trophies.

And no one checked up on the purchase of that particular gun—ever—and five more women would die before Kemper turned himself in, paying for the toll calls himself.

In his confession, he told the Santa Cruz County law enforcement officers, "The fact that you didn't ask for that .22 is one of the reasons that I blew it this last week. I was getting very paranoid about that."

"All right," said Lieutenant Scherer. "Where did you pick up Cindy?"

"It was on Mission," said the Confessor. "I was cruising around, close on five o'clock or so. I had been cruising around the campus (UCSC) and I'd picked up three different girls, two of them together, that were possibilities, but I cancelled those out because there were too many people standing around that possibly knew them when they got in. But all the other conditions were perfect.

"It had been drizzling, it had been raining real hard, and people were getting any ride they could get, and windows were fogging up. Nobody was paying any attention, and it was during that real heavy rain. But I had given up on those other two and I was kind of uptight about it; and driving down the street, I spotted her standing out there with her thumb out."

Scherer asked for a physical description.

"A large girl," Kemper recalled. "She was, I think, five-foot-four inches, maybe one-hundred-sixty pounds, straight, medium-long blonde hair, and very large chested—uh, breasted, I should say."

He described her brocaded blouse, her man's woolen work shirt, and a blue plastic waterproof jacket. She had also worn brown corduroy bell bottoms and hiking boots. The shirt, which was checked, he decided to keep in his own closet since it was large and resembled some shirts he had inherited from his brother-in-law's father. It was safer, he felt, too, than throwing things into the Good Will hampers. Cindy wore the little home-made ring and two very plain gold wire earrings for pierced ears. The ring he kept for quite a while. These souvenirs were important props in his fantasy world.

He was astounded at how quickly he killed Cindy.

He had driven her to the little town of Freedom near Watsonville and then into the hills and up a sideroad. They talked.

"I was playing a little game of not blowing it, you know. Somebody's going to talk with me or, you know, that's it, by God. So I said, you know, I convinced her that I don't like guns and all that, it was just bull, and that I wasn't going to use it, and I just nonchalantly tucked it away under my leg there and didn't refer to it again until later. And now and then I picked it up and played around with it, but did everything but hand it to her. To calm her down. Several times she asked me not to kill her and it got to the point later on it was very nonchalant. . . . Lying through my teeth."

The sadistic cat-and-mouse game, the reveling in momentary power, were fundamental and crucial to Kemper's triumph. Cindy did not take kindly to his suggestion that she climb into the trunk. He convinced her that he would take her to his mother's house where they could talk, but that it would be better if she were not seen in the car by nosey neighbors.

The girl was distressed about missing her class and losing her grade, since she said her parents would then cease supporting her college education. But Kemper talked her into the trunk finally and arranged the blanket as a pillow.

At first the gun confused him for it had a two-stage trigger pull. He squeezed the trigger. She looked around just through the corner of her eye and caught him with the gun up, then quickly turned toward him. He squeezed again.

"There was no jerk," Kemper said, referring to the motion of the girl's body. "Every other case there has always been at least, you know, a jerk, a little reflex. There was absolutely nothing . . . She followed through with the motion."

The bullet had lodged in her skull.

"Just like, it amazed me so much because one second she's animated and the next second she's not, and there was absolutely nothing between. Just a noise and absolute, absolute stillness." The time was a quarter of nine.

He covered her body in the trunk with the blanket and began to drive to his mother's house.

The fresh cast on his arm, he noticed, was now spattered with new blood. At home he would have to put white shoe polish on it.

When he arrived at Clarnell Strandberg's green duplex, he noticed with pleasure that the neighbors were not at home. And the weather was drizzly. Perfect. The girl's weight in the trunk of the car was causing it to sag a little. He feared that his mother would arrive home momentarily. Hurry!

With difficulty, because of his bad arm, he carried her into the house, placed her body in his closet, and closed the sliding door. Soon afterward, his mother returned home.

He talked with her for a time and then went to bed. Kemper could hardly wait until next morning and his mother's departure for work.

No sooner had she gone than he carried Cynthia's body into his bedroom and engaged in sex acts. Afterward he dissected it, using at times his old Division of Highways axe. He meticulously removed the shower curtains in the bathtub before beginning his grisly task and afterward washed away all traces of the blood. Later he discarded the axe at the Santa Cruz Dump.

Placing the remains in plastic sacks, he drove down the coast into Monterey County and threw parts of the body off a cliff south of Carmel. Some of these were discovered the very next day, while others were returned by the ocean to Santa Cruz. He was worried about getting rid of the body because the ground was damp and the tracks of his size fifteen shoes were clear in it. He erased them as best he could. He also seriously considered getting his tires recapped for the same reason. Because of the danger of identification, he buried her head in the back yard at his mother's home.

Very late at night he drove north with Cynthia's clothing to the town of Alameda, where he stopped at a deserted laundromat. He put her coat into a dryer, turned it on full hot, and placed four dimes in the slot. The heat, he calculated, would ruin the inexpensive garment.

"I figured it would melt certain spots of the plastic and the owner would come in—he's a little old black guy—and he'd get pissed and throw it in the garbage."

When the killer checked back that morning between 5:00 and 6:00 o'clock, he discovered that that was exactly what had happened.

His interrogators wanted more details and Kemper was happy to oblige. As to the dissection, he had also used a knife. "I used the same knife in all of them. It's a buck knife; it's called the General; and it's the largest. It's something like a Bowie knife, but it has more of a straight blade, rather than real fancy or curved."

When not using it, he kept it at home in a black case inside a pink chest of drawers, which was where he also kept his arsenal of guns, pistols, and ammunition. As to this knife, he had gone to a great deal of trouble to sharpen it, for it was of extremely hard tempered steel. He explained the procedure carefully. (A moment later, being questioned by Lieutenant Scherer, he contradicted his earlier statement and said he had not used this knife on Mary Ann and Anita—that had been his pocket knife.)

He told how the discovery of Cindy's body less than twenty-four hours after he had disposed of it had alarmed him greatly —not only because she was the first of his victims to be found thus far, but because at that time he still had her head in a box in his closet. And at any moment, he feared, officers would appear at the door to question him.

"It quite noticeably shocked me when I heard on the radio, the very next day after depositing the body over the cliff, that it had been discovered," he said. And he had gone straight into the back yard and buried the head, even though he feared that the police might then be watching the house and his every move.

Sergeant Aluffi wanted to know why Kemper had chosen the campus area for picking up girls.

"Well, I didn't actually," Kemper said. "At first that was one of my rules, don't ever hit around town, but then, sometime after that (I don't remember whether it was after the first two, or the third one, Aiko) Mary was abducted and disappeared, apparently, from what I read in the paper . . . And I couldn't see someone—like the paper said—of her apparent background disappearing like that when they're going to college. So I assumed that someone else was doing the same thing I was doing, and they had hit in town, and that kind of made me mad because that could throw everything in my lap if an investigation started around Santa Cruz. Because up until that point, I had assumed that the authorities were looking for someone in the Bay Area that was depositing the heads in the Santa Cruz area. . . .

"When I was disabled and staying with my mother, when I first started to live with her, when I . . . realized that no investigation was coming my way at all, I realized that I was being a little too careful. And there was a much better opportunity around the Santa Cruz area to attack these coeds. I had been hitting primarily the Berkeley area . . . the University of California, and I saw no reason to ease my—completely leave out Santa Cruz as long as I was careful.

"So this is why I started out with the Cabrillo school; it was quite by accident. I had been looking for University coeds when I picked up Cindy. I kind of picked her up as an afterthought. I was pretty pleased."

Just before that, however, he had picked up two University girls on the UCSC campus, planning to tell them they were being abducted—but found he was afraid.

"I guess I just emotionally wasn't quite prepared to jump anybody," he said, "and they were quite beautiful girls, and the opportunity was so great and everything; it just caught me off guard. Before I knew it, I was dropping them off, and apparently they lived on Locust Street where Alice, a later victim, also lived."

He had then circled back through the campus but had found no one else "readily available" for a "hit."

As he drove back down Mission toward the center of town, fate had presented the figure of Cynthia. And this first hit inside town proved so gratifying that he moved ahead at once with his plans to strike on the University campus.

CHAPTER THIRTEEN

UNDER MOTHER'S WINDOW

THE EVENING OF February 5 was again good hunting weather, being rainy. And Kemper was in a rage.

"My mother and I," he said, "had had a real tiff . . . I told her I was going to a movie, and I jumped up and went straight to the campus because it was still early.

"I said, the first girl that's halfway decent that I pick up, I'm gonna blow her brains out."

Another point was in his favor as he entered the campus at around 8:30. A lecture had been scheduled that was attracting many cars. He always worried about the guards in the kiosks, even with his parking sticker, because of the badly crushed rear fender with the "Mickey Mouse-type taillight wired on it, which is extremely noticeable and easy to remember."

But the guard just waved him on by. When he had gotten the parking sticker from his mother, he explained to the investigators, he had done so deliberately "for the purpose of doing things like that. I told her I wanted to be able to go up there and park, and go into the library, and drive through and park where I wanted to."

Mrs. Strandberg, accommodating her offspring, had regarded it as a small cost for restoring peace in the family. And there *had* been peace in her life, briefly, until Edmund returned.

Rosalind, 23, was a big, usually happy, girl who had entered the University right after graduating from high school in 1968. The campus reflected her love for her coastal hometown, the trees, the clean air off the ocean, the beaches, the good life. And for her the future was promising. She was almost finished with her academic work at Merrill College.

She emerged into the rain from her evening class just as Kemper drove past. He noted, even in the poor visibility, that her hair was "light brown with blondish tints," that she was wearing "black felt bell-bottom sailor pants, pink-and-purple zip-up boots," and that she was carrying a purse with a strap.

"I said, well, she's not too bad looking. So I stopped and she hesitated—she was probably twenty yards behind the car—and looked to the rear, and she saw the wrecked-up car there and hesitated for a moment. Then," he continued, "I'm sure that she saw the A tag, and ran right along and hopped in . . .

"She asked me where I was going. And that had always been a problem with me, because when they ask me where I'm going and I say the wrong thing, they won't get in. If I say I'm going down Mission and they say they're going up the other end of Mission or something like this, sometimes it's an excuse not to get in. Sometimes they're going the other way, and I'll blow an awful good opportunity 'cause I don't think quick enough."

As Kemper began this recital, technology interrupted the flow. The tape ran out. While he and the officers waited for the recorder to be reloaded, he raised a concern as to how the tapes would be used—whether they would be played in the courtroom or presented as typewritten transcripts.

"I asked the sergeant this morning especially about that," he said, "because that's an awful touchy thing where the family's involved, and I'm being very frank here, and it's going to be hard enough as it is there, and I'm sure that parents should be talked to. I wouldn't even attempt to approach any of them. I doubt that any of them would be anywhere near me as far as wanting to ask me anything.

"Having been through that type of situation with my uncle, with my grandparents there the first time I was in court." (At fifteen, Edmund had been deeply hurt by the reaction of a favorite uncle to his first murders.) "It's an awfully touchy subject, you know, what happened and what didn't happen, and some of these things that did happen which you know weren't all that bad; still it's going to be awfully terrible for the family to have to listen to this . . . I've heard of things like where certain tapes are played just in front of the judge, or just in front of the jury, as evidence rather than play it in front of the whole court because I—that, that starts to look like an arena, you know, and everything is in there . . . all the gory details. That would get me very upset, and I'd probably ask to leave the court and the judge would say, no, you're going to sit there and listen, and then I'd start throwing chairs and having a fit, scream on the floor and all that stuff."

More to the point, Job knew what had happened to the Christians when they were thrown into the arena. He had just succeeded in surrendering by long-distance telephone. Now if only the trial could be conducted with the defendant or the victims' families *in absentia*.

And Job, at that moment, knew better than anyone else the full extent of his atrocities. The truth would almost literally be dragged from him by the Public Defender's staff in the hope of finding evidence to support the plea of not guilty by reason of insanity.

But the stolid Lieutenant Scherer, his tape reloaded, was not to be diverted by delicate considerations.

"All right," he said. "Let's go into Rosalind here. You had her in the car. What was your next move?"

As with all his intended victims, Kemper had started talking with her.

"Basically," he said, "she carried the conversation. She was very outgoing and I was just trying to be amicable, and I was trying to think of what I was gonna do. I had decided, after we rode a little ways, that that was it. I was gonna get her, definitely, and I had my little *zapple!* through my body there that always confirmed it. I never had one of those where it didn't actually happen. It's just where everything would click just right; circumstances were perfect. Nobody else was around, the guard didn't notice me coming in, nothing would look unusual going out, and she was not the least bit suspecting.

"And, also, it was somebody I didn't know in any way, shape, or form, or knew anybody that I knew about . . . Those were certain things I held as absolutes. One I had held as an absolute for a long time was, don't ever do anything like that around the Santa Cruz area because that's too close to home, and having been in the past I was in, I would naturally come under suspicion. But then I started getting sicker and sicker later on and a little more and more careless in my approach, in taking care of things, and afterwards—which I'm sure got obvious, because more and more evidence started popping up, in different forms.

"Okay, what happened next is, we were talking and she's more or less popping little questions here and there, talking along. I noticed Alice standing on the side. She saw us coming, threw out a great big beautiful smile, and stuck her thumb out very helpfully, and you know, not a cheesecake-type thing, but you know, throwing her best foot forward there. I figure later on what happened was, that she looked to me from just different little details, that she was probably a careful hitchhiker. Very good looking, built nicely and everything, and intelligent and moderate in her dress and everything, nothing outlandish.

"From some of her I.D., college friends, stable background, and all that, I imagine she was a cautious hitchhiker, and she always made sure of her ride before she got in, and we appeared to be a couple, and with that A tag on there . . . So she didn't hesitate at all about getting in."

He had been relieved to note that the girls did not know each other. As the car approached the kiosk on the way out, "I was very careful in eyeballing the guard as I went by, and he glanced, and I'm sure he didn't see Alice in the back seat because of the lighting and the fact that her clothes were dark, except for the top, light-colored tweed peacoat."

Alice, he said, was five-feet-two and, "It surprised me, her being an Oriental, that she was built like she was. Nothing fantastic, I mean, but you know, very nice build. Anyway, she had long, black hair, rather coarse, and very square sort of a face, very wide, high cheekbones."

Her costume, quickly "eyeballed" by Edmund Kemper, consisted of suede desert boots, Levi bell bottoms, with a wide brown belt that fitted stylishly and becomingly around her hips, which appealed to him at once. She wore "a supporting bra to accentuate her figure" beneath her light-blue turtleneck sweater with a zipper in the back, and an old gray peacoat over this; and her socks were bright red.

The inventorying eye also registered the fact that Alice was carrying a purple book bag with white Chinese lettering on the front. Soon it was learned that her wallet contained a lot of I.D. cards, pictures, and things like that.

As for the other girl, "What struck me about Rosalind was that she didn't have any money at all, not even change in her purse. She had just gotten a letter from home with a check in it."

"Where's the check?" asked Scherer.

"At the bottom of the ocean." But for a time Kemper had kept all these things, worrying as to whether the police might descend on the house, or whether his mother might go through his closet, "and immediately know what it was without even opening it"—meaning, book bag and purse.

So he had gone down the coast below Carmel, out past "that Rocky Creek point" on the way to Big Sur, and had thrown the girls' bags over the cliff. But that was in mid-April. He had not been able to part with them for several weeks.

"What happened," asked Lieutenant Scherer, determined to

keep the trolley on the tracks, "when you had both girls in the car, now?"

Well, they had gotten past the campus guard. Kemper and Rosalind were chatting. Alice sat quietly in the back seat. As they went down around the first curve of the broad new road from the campus to where it straightened out and where the city lights became visible, Kemper commented on the beautiful view. He slowed down, asking Rosalind if she minded. She said, "Not at all." Alice in back also said she did not mind, but Kemper got the feeling she was just saying it to be polite, and that she was beginning to feel disgusted. He was hypersensitive to the opinion of the lovely creature in the back seat, knowing instinctively that such a woman could never love a fellow like him. He was watching, however, for cars either coming or going. He was hesitating, scared.

"I had never done something like that before," he said, "where I just come out and shot somebody, just right out in the blue. But I was mad that night."

Kemper mad, as it turned out, was just about the same, operationally, as Kemper benevolent—as when he had picked up Mary Ann, Anita, Aiko, and Cynthia.

He considered having picked up two girls as a remarkable improvement on his initial humble ambitions for the evening. "As it was, I improved. It was two in a perfect situation . . .

"Anyway, we slowed down there, almost to a stop. We were just barely moving and I had been moving my pistol from down below my leg in my lap, a solid black pistol, and the interior of the car was black, so she couldn't see it and I picked it up and had it in my lap, talking with them; and I moved it up to the side like this, I just picked it up and pulled the trigger, 'cause I knew the minute I picked it up like that, the girl in the back was gonna see it and I didn't want any problems. So as soon as I picked it up, I hesitated maybe a second at the very most, and then pulled the trigger."

The car was moving very slowly.

"Like, I didn't want the brake lights on in case somebody was around the corner, 'cause that would be something to stick in their memory."

Careful, careful Edmund, always premeditating. A district attorney would have to be incompetent to avoid getting him on Murder One.

As he lifted the gun up, Rosalind started to turn her head. Alice gasped. He pulled the trigger. Rosalind instantly fell over against the window. The bullet had entered just above her left ear.

"She had a rather large forehead and I was imagining what her brain looked like inside, and I just wanted to put it right in the middle of that."

Even in the dark, in an awkward position, he handled the gun like a brain surgeon's scalpel, earning another Dennison's gold star to paste on his pistol.

Alice covered her face with her hands and ducked into a corner of the back seat. In the final moment of her life, where else was there to go? Kemper shot through her hands, missing twice. A third shot "hit her just right around the temple area . . ." (The exact, detailed course of the bullet was described.) He shot her several more times.

She was unconscious, "But she was making a very strange sound. I almost threw up as we were going down the hill. It was a sigh. A constant, over and over, sigh."

Lieutenant Scherer asked him to describe the shooting again, and he obliged in detail. "With her, I fired the first time and it went through her hand. She was moving around quite rapidly, trying to get away from the gun because I had to fire right-handed because of the cast. Otherwise, in both cases I would have fired left-handed. It was awkward in both cases. I had to turn around like this, so I was at a bad angle with her and I missed. They were bad shots the first two times. But the third shot, I moved it almost out of my hand and around at a direct angle. The first shot through her hand missed her completely, and the second one grazed her head and also went through her hand, and embedded itself in the car, and ricocheted back out the front. Then the third shot, I was positive that she was unconscious, I don't really think I needed to do that.

"She was very slumped over in the seat and she was

scrunched way down . . . So her head was not visible above
the cushion like it normally would be. So I just put the coat
over her, grabbed the blanket, and unfolded it enough—and I
tried to push Rosalind over into the floorboard area, and she
wouldn't budge. She was just sitting there, slumped over completely. And so finally I just pulled her over sideways on the
seat and put the blue velveteen sort of blanket over her and
made sure it stayed below the level of the windows there and
that it wasn't an obvious shape or anything. I kept it double
thickness, and just opened it enough so it looked like a flat
blue surface."

He continued down the hill, never hitting the brakes.

"Right after I put the blanket over her, a car came down. I
smoothly accelerated so there wouldn't be a blast of gas and a
jerk or anything. So I am sure that to them it appeared as if I
was just cruising along. They came down behind us, and I
came right down in front of the guard station at the bottom
where the cars were parked and everything. And there were
two guards standing right by the road out there, having a
little conversation. They were, maybe, twenty feet from the car,
on their side of the car."

Scherer asked if Alice were moaning or gasping then.

"Yeah, it was a sigh, a very strange sigh. It would start out
very sharp, almost like a sniffle, and then it would taper off
and become a little bit more like a masculine sigh than (from)
a fine girl, a petite-type girl like she was. It wasn't low or anything, but it was very disconcerting and it was constant. After
we stopped, and went on down Bay Street, obviously there was
quite a bit of blood because of the wounds, and there was
blood from that last hole in the forehead."

Kemper proceeded straight down to Mission, turned right,
and headed out of town.

"I was making sure that I broke absolutely no rules and was
doing my damnedest to look cool while I was freaking out
about Alice in the back seat there, which I am sure she was
unconscious. At first I didn't think so and I made a couple of
loud statements, and it just continued right on through, so I

knew she was unconscious. But the blood started running and started gurgling, and the sighing was still there. So as soon as I got out to the edge of town, I stepped on the gas and got the hell away from there, and a little further down the road, where no cars were coming, I slowed down very slow, turned her head around to the side, and fired point-blank at the side of her head.

"The reason she didn't go instantly like the other girl was that the automatic had a kind of quirky ramp, and it would not—you couldn't load all the points into the clip, or I would have always used those. I could only put one in the barrel and nine regular solid-head long rifles in the clip, and everything I fired at her was solids. So one solid slug she got in there—and she was doing the moaning. I got out of town and turned her head to the side and fired point-blank, and the flash was so great that I could see some of the tissue coming out. She stopped immediately. There was silence, and then I turned back around about two seconds later and it started up again, and it was really getting to me.

"There's a place down the road, you know, that popular beach area where the sign is, like where it says Davenport, Bonny Doon, and all that? A lot of people park there. Well, the next one back from there is the loop. Some people get on that and think they're going to Bonny Doon, and it loops right back out. Laguna. I circled back down through that and went up on that little cul-de-sac up in there and parked. I had the parking lights on. I jumped out and put both of them in the trunk."

With his injured arm, he had great difficulty with Rosalind, who was heavy. And in dragging Alice around to the trunk, he lost one of his size fifteen shoes. He retrieved it quickly.

A blue plastic laundry bag with blood on it blew under the car. He got down, fished it out, and put it back in. (When it rained later that night, he felt greatly relieved.)

With the bodies in the trunk, he drove back to Santa Cruz, stopping at the Fast Gas station on the left.

"There was a Chinese girl pumping gas. I went into the

rest room and cleaned off as much of the blood on the cast as I could, and I cleaned a little off my pants. To myself I called them my murder clothes because it was those dark pants; they were a dark blue denim Western style pants with very light, not quite white, markings. But they were very dark. That was in case I got them splattered. I used them on the first two girls. I think I used them when Aiko and Cynthia were killed. I am not sure, but in the vast majority of the cases I used those pants and shirt."

The shirt, with some rusty looking stains on it, still hung in his closet at home.

Kemper remained at the gas station for quite a while, talking to the Chinese girl, and as he put it, "acting nonchalant." Then he went home and talked to his mother a little, crabbing about how he had fallen asleep in the movie. He said, "How do you like that? You go and pay all that money and then fall asleep." (And, asleep, you could not be expected to remember the plot.) "Then I said I would go back and see it tomorrow night, and that gives me an alibi."

Still acting nonchalant, Kemper observed that he needed cigarettes and left the house.

"The way the house is laid out, there's a big picture window that's enclosed with curtains, and the TV is right over here against the wall, and my mother sits right where that picture window is. All she would have to do is get up and take a couple of steps and open the curtain in order to see if I am still out there; and she hadn't heard the car leave. But what I didn't realize was that she wouldn't hear that over the TV. So I just went out there, pulled the car around and opened up the trunk, and this is the way the entire series happened. I took out that big knife and I cut both of their heads right off out there on the street.

"It was maybe ten o'clock at night, or possibly eleven. But that's where I did that because of the blood problem. Because they both had bled very badly in the trunk during the time of riding around and sitting at the gas station. It was getting all over everything. Then I went down and got my cigarettes at this little bar down by Seacliff, walked back out, got in the car, and drove home and went back into the house and watched TV and went to bed. The next day my mother was at work, and it was drizzling, and I just backed up . . ."

Lieutenant Scherer asked Kemper to hold it a minute while they changed the tape.

The girls' clothing had been drenched with a tremendous amount of blood, as if it had been sponges, a fact that surprised him. But on the following morning he carried Alice into his mother's house, right in through the back door. "Because I knew the old biddy in the back there never was out in the rain, so I just wandered on in there and committed this act, which was actually rather difficult. And actually I think that being the last time I did anything like that. It was rather distasteful. I guess maybe the first time I did something like that, there was a little bit of a charge, you know. But that time—"

Rosalind's body remained in the trunk, although he took her head into the house the following day and removed the bullet from it—again, as he said, and may have believed, to avoid the tracing of it.

"I cleaned the blood off both of them in the bathroom . . . so I wouldn't get all bloody." Then he placed Alice's body on the floor and engaged in sexual intercourse with it. He did not sever her hands until he had taken her back to the car, explaining, "It was an afterthought." He also endeavored to wash her body to conceal the evidence of his necrophilia.

More trouble with the tape recorder interrupted his confession. Kemper observed to Lieutenant Scherer, "This is kind of bad tonight 'cause you remind me a lot of my father. I've never met you personally, or seen you personally. My first impression was—my father's taller, but you have a lot of his features. So that makes it rather, uh, macabre here. A John Wayne image of my father . . . so anybody that looks like him, I immediately cast him as a father hero."

Lieutenant Scherer chose not to respond.

Kemper continued. "This is a bummer. Which is why I get depressed in that damn cell 'cause I realized earlier today after talking to you guys that I do not—I make a very strong attempt not to think about any of this stuff, anything related to it, and especially my mother while I'm in that cell, because I just get super depressed. I'm just sitting there. I still haven't slept in four days. I tried two more times back there to sleep, and I'd lay down—and the first thing, I'd start thinking about this last weekend. And I get super torqued-up and I'm wide awake; just absolutely not drowsy. And this is including 1,500 miles of driving almost constantly, and the last nine hundred miles of it was nothing but gas—a bottle of pop once in a while, and a lot of No-Doz."

He started talking about his youth, but the machine was still malfunctioning, so part of the record was inaudible. "Before I got into that trouble when I was fifteen, I . . . and ever after that I got in trouble . . . was one very hard point of consternation. It had a lot to do with my getting upset with society and deciding to attack. It was that I was frustrated in my dreams and desires totally. It was sad, really. I didn't blame society for me not being able to be a policeman, but—"

At this point Edmund the Confessor descended to his cop-buttering, maudlin best. Again Scherer stolidly, like some uniformed Powerful Katrinka, set the trolley right back on the track.

"All right," he said. "Now, we've got Alice in your room. Now, what happened after the sexual act?"

Kemper explained that this was early afternoon and that he could hear signs of a party going on upstairs. He simply carried the mutilated corpse, wrapped casually in a blanket, weighing almost nothing and feeling like a mannequin. "I just wandered right out there with her and put her in the trunk right under the window.

"That's one thing that amazes me about society. That is, that you can do damn near anything and nobody's gonna say anything or notice."

He decided to do no further dismembering of the bodies because of the difficulties presented.

"At that point, I was just not caring if somebody finds those portions of their bodies, but hoping that it would be at least a few days . . ."

He then drove to Alameda to visit an old friend, indicating to the officers that this was a woman. The only woman he was ever seen with, however, was his alleged fiancée, the young girl from the Valley, whom he had said down at the Jury Room on one occasion that he might marry.

"I went up and visited that friend—a good friend of mine, up there, that lived in the same neighborhood as I did when I worked with the state, and I dropped by and I was fairly agitated that night, and she noticed it. I was kidding around a lot and was very nervous. My stomach was killing me. I think I'm developing ulcers because of all this. Not so much now, but I was in a great tension whenever something like that was happening, especially people in the trunk and having to dispose . . . I'd get close to the point of panic until it was done. Then I would just completely relax. But this tension would just build and build to the point of removal of the bodies; and I'll tell you, on that road, Eden Road there—"

It had rained that afternoon as he drove up Highway 17 to the Bay Area. This choice was based on the fact that the girls were from Santa Cruz and, "I wanted to distract the heat from Santa Cruz. So I figured I knew both areas, and the authorities wouldn't necessarily know that I knew the Bay Area well, because the job that I do entails intensive travel through those areas. Especially like with the disposal of Alice's head and hands, I knew that this was an ideal place because the authorities would figure it was somebody that knew that particular area really well, and I knew that people at two o'clock in the morning would not be traveling the road at all. So they would think it would be at least somebody within five or ten miles of that area, and that's what I wanted people to think."

After visiting the friend, he went to dinner, which he found himself unable to eat, went to a movie, again refueled his gas-guzzling car—stalling for time to make sure he would be late.

"I arrived on the scene up in Eden Canyon Road about

two A.M." He began looking for suitable disposal sites, shining his big, powerful flashlight around. No cars came along. Finally, he removed both bodies from the trunk and rolled them over the edge of the road. He was carrying the heads and the hands in a red plastic dishpan in his car. So now he decided to turn and drive across to San Francisco, then south again along the coast to Pacifica—a town set in hills which resemble the Scottish Highlands. On the ocean side of the highway, cliffs drop down sheer to the beach. Kemper drove to an area known as Devil's Slide.

It looked good, but he took the precaution of cruising through the town of Pacifica itself. He noticed that the local patrolmen were having coffee at a shop there. This was good. Returning to Devil's Slide, he threw his parcels over the cliff.

But later, as usual, he got to worrying. It wasn't that alone, however, which drew the necrophile back to the scene. Still, he felt he had done a stupid thing, throwing the heads down there.

Later he wondered, "Why didn't I just bury them somewhere?" But again he had been too "torqued-up" and wanted no more problem of hassling bodies. Two weeks later, he returned to check. It was about four o'clock in the morning, and he made a stealthy predator's examination of the embankment.

There was good reason for stealth. The investigation now ranged across four counties. Public reaction had become hysterical. Cynthia's body had been positively identified on January 24. Mary's body was found February 11. The vanishing of Alice and Rosalind was announced in the papers on February 8. And the day after the UC student body combed the woods for the latter on the fourteenth, two California Division of Highways workmen (Kemper's sometime colleagues) discovered two headless female bodies thirty feet off the Eden Valley Road near Highway 580 in Alameda county. And on the twentieth, they were positively identified as those of Alice and Rosalind. Just the week before, Herbert Mullin had been arrested—but with the judicial gag order in effect, the public had no knowledge of whether other killers remained at large.

Because Cynthia's Achilles tendons had been severed, there was further speculation that the killer or killers had professional medical skill. (Kemper was angered by this report, because it implied that he was a butcher, when in fact he had severed the tendons only because rigor mortis had set in while the body was still in the trunk.)

In the predawn, he flashed his light along the embankment and as far down as he could see. Everything looked all right, Kemper got back in his car and continued on up the coast. He was due at Kaiser Hospital to get his cast changed.

On the UC campus they held a memorial service in an old limestone quarry that formed a natural amphitheater. Up through the mist and the redwoods trudged students and faculty to pay their last respects to the memories of Rosalind and Alice. Robert Edgar, provost of Kresge College where Alice had been a student, recited a Haiku poem that would have served as an appropriate memorial for each of Edmund Kemper's young victims:

> *She was bright and lovely*
> *Like a bird she was full of song*
> *Now she has been struck down*
> *And I am full of grief.*

Later, each of the families of the murdered girls held memorial services in their own fashion and in their own communities. But in some cases, as with Aiko's mother, it was months before the fact of death could be accepted.

Beyond the white sands and inky surf of the Monterey Peninsula, on a day like other days with the gulls crying and the pungency of kelp filling the air and a flight of Arctic terns rising like the strophe of a choral ode, they scattered the ashes of Rosalind. She had walked on these beaches as a child and an adolescent, returning to them as a university student, and they said it was what she had wished.

CHAPTER FOURTEEN

"NICE" BEHEADING FOR MOM

EASTER WEEKEND. The hour of 4:00 A.M.

"I laid there in the bed thinking about it. And it's something hard to just up and do. It was the most insane of reasons for going and killing your mother. But I was pretty fixed on that issue because there were a lot of things involved. Someone just standing off to the side, watching, isn't really going to see any kind of sense, or rhyme or reason . . .

"I had done some things, and I felt that I had to carry the full weight of everything that happened. I certainly wanted for my mother a nice, quiet, easy death like I guess everyone wants."

Edmund therefore resolved upon the nicest way of executing it. He waited until 5:15 A.M.

"I went into the kitchen and got a hammer. We have a regular claw hammer at home. I picked up my pocket knife, the same one I had used to kill Mary Ann with, opened it up, and I carried that in my right hand and the hammer in my left, and I walked into her bedroom very quietly. She had been sound asleep. She moved around a little bit, and I thought maybe she was waking up. I just waited and waited and she was just laying there.

"So I approached her right side . . . I stood there a couple of minutes, I suppose, and I hit her just above the temple on her right side of the head . . . It was above and behind her temple on the right side of her head. I struck with a very hard blow, and I believe I dropped the hammer, or I laid it down, or something.

"Immediately after striking that blow I looked for a reaction, and there really wasn't one. Blood started running down her face from the wound, and she was still breathing. I could hear the breathing. And I heard blood running into her; I guess it was her windpipe. It was obvious I had done severe damage to her, because in other cases where I had shot people in the head I heard the same—or it had the same effect—blood running into the breathing passages. And this all happened in a few seconds."

The Confessor described with his usual passion for detail how he had moved his mother over on her back, held her chin up with his right hand, and slashed her throat. She bled profusely. This was when he decided, "What's good for my victims was good for my mother," so he did not stop with the throat but went the rest of the way around her neck and took off her head. He figured the whole slaughtering took less than half a minute, for by now, he was extremely dexterous.

He moved her out of the bed, not wanting to leave a big mess that family members might notice if they dropped in, and put his handcuffs on her wrists because it was hard to drag her body into the closet. He turned over the mattress and cleaned blood off the wall and elsewhere, including the carpet. It was now well into the morning and the house looked back to normal.

In this preliminary confession, Kemper told less than all of his morning's activities. The ultimate horrors were never divulged, either to his attorney or to the prosecutor, until a special psychiatric questioning occurred under the influence of "truth serum."

He said he had become quite ill immediately after killing his mother and had eaten nothing the night before.

"I couldn't stand being around the house anymore."

He put his guns into his car and started driving around town. He was looking for a hardware store where he wanted to buy a hacksaw blade. He was also in the market for a new sidearm and thought of cutting down his carbine and making it into a semi-pistol automatic weapon.

While cruising around, he ran into an acquaintance, Robert McFadzen, who owed him $10.00 and who Kemper thought had been avoiding him for that reason. He could not help "chortling" though at what McFadzen did not know—which was that he had buried little Aiko's torso behind his chum's house. Even in the worst of times, Kemper could enjoy a flash of wry humor.

He spotted McFadzen driving down Forty-first Avenue. "I pulled up behind and gave him my up-and-down beams. He didn't immediately recognize my car until I hit the light, because I didn't have my whip antenna on the car."

McFadzen pulled over and they both proceeded into a Sears Roebuck parking lot. They decided to go have breakfast, which meant, Kemper said, "Let's go get drunk." He got into his friend's car and they drove to a liquor store where McFadzen cashed a check.

"And there he offered me the ten dollars, which to tell you the truth, saved his life, because with his little excuses, I needed to kill somebody at that point, and I think he deserved it more than anybody. He offered me the ten dollars without my having to mention it, so I just took five dollars of it and figured we'd drink on the other five."

Kemper also meant to cash some checks that day, overdrawing his account, because he wanted money for the getaway.

After the two men had several drinks, they went to Gray's Gun Shop for the purpose of Kemper's either buying or renting one of the owner's personal sidearms. But the proprietor turned them down flat, citing his license regulations.

Then Kemper telephoned another acquaintance, hoping to borrow his pistol, but got no answer. At that point he left McFadzen, saying he would see him the following weekend—which he had no intention of doing.

He returned to the house for a couple of hours, frantically trying to think of a course of action. He realized that the absence of his mother on Easter Sunday would alarm the family, as would her failure to appear at work on Monday morning.

"I decided that someone else had to die too, a friend of hers, as a cover-up, an excuse; something that would be believable by other people and friends and possible family that might get in touch. So I started thinking about who would be a victim; who would be most available; who would be the easiest to kill; and who would be likely to be gone with my mother for the weekend. I fell upon a friend of hers, Sara or Sally Hallett, who had frequently gone places with my mother and done things on weekends.

"There was another friend, Mrs. Victoria Sims, who would have been just as easy if not for the fact that she was married and was with her husband for the weekend, and possibly with her daughter and her daughter's boy friend. So that completely ruled that person out because it was too involved."

He tried to call Mrs. Hallett's home telephone, which was unlisted, getting the number from his mother's personal book. There was no answer.

Kemper called several times that Saturday afternoon, then went out again. He was worried that Sally might have gone somewhere for the weekend, perhaps with her son. He drank beer and sat around the house. Then he got in his mother's car, drove it to a street in an area where his family or their friends would be unlikely to visit, parked it, and took the keys home. He drank more beer. Mrs. Hallett telephoned around five-thirty and asked to speak to his mother.

Kemper, before telling her that his mother was not at home, said he had just gone back to work, had gotten a raise while he was home recuperating for four-and-a-half months with his broken arm, and that he was celebrating.

He asked her to join him and his mother for dinner and a movie, which was to surprise his mother.

"The reason I did this," he said, "was I knew she'd accept . . . I had surmised from past acquaintance with her at home and out that she would leap at something like that, so that's what I thought to say. Of course she jumped at the idea. I told her that my mother was not home but would be a little later." He urged Sara Hallett to come over at about seven-thirty and she said, "Fine."

Kemper, his heart thumping, began at once to prepare for her. First, he closed all the windows and doors in the house to make sure not only that sound could not carry outside, but that the bedrooms were screened from view. This made the living room seem very quiet.

He still had the strong nylon rope-cord that he had taken from Mary Ann and Anita, and he placed it in the living room. He also brought out a drill shank he had taken from his high-ways job, a broken piece of equipment that would make a fine bludgeon. His carbine he placed in the next room against a wall—"just in case." He had decided that "one shot was better than a lot of screaming, in case something went wrong where she was lucky and possibly incapacitated me partially."

It was very quiet in the neighborhood that day: apparently the neighbors were away. Sally was late arriving. When she finally came, it was almost eight o'clock. Edmund met her at the door, greeting her with his usual courtesy and warmth, and removing her wrap, which was a sweater.

They talked about where his mother might be, and Kemper said he felt sure she would be along soon, that she had just called from a friend's house. Sally accepted this fully. They moved together across the living room toward the couch.

Kemper was remembering the three-inch medical tapes that he had used in the Aiko killing, and which now were stuck lightly onto the kitchen wall, just around the corner from the living room. He had also brought two clear plastic bags into the house. His handcuffs were in his pocket. The stage was as set as it would ever be.

"So anyway she came and we talked, and we were crossing the living room towards the couch. I was balking at what I had to do or what I felt I had to do, and that was the last thing I wanted to do. I didn't want to seem obvious at anything being wrong. I was stalling around as we moved across the room. My first intention was to strike her in the midsection, around the solar plexus, and knock the wind from her so that she couldn't cry out, and then strangle her. It was this first move that I was kind of dreading. I guess what worked me into it really quick was that she said, 'Let's sit down. I'm dead.'

"And I kind of took her at her word there. I guess I saw that as a cue, and I struck her in the stomach. She fell back or jumped back mostly, I guess. I was quite surprised at her reaction. I hit her hard, and she jumped back and said, "Guy, stop that." I struck her again immediately after the first blow, and her last words were, "Oh!" and she stumbled back. I pulled her around toward me, facing away from me, threw my left arm around her neck. It was hurting at that point, but I didn't realize it then because I was so wrapped up in what I was doing.

"It's almost like a blacking out. You know what you're doing but you don't notice anything else around. But in striking her, I had held my thumb wrong when I made a fist, and had jammed my thumb and hurt my wrist. It's weak anyway, being in a cast so long. But I grabbed her around the neck with the left wrist at her throat, put her to a choke hold, and pulled her up off the floor. In fact, she was dangling across my chest, with absolutely no sounds coming from her. She was holding my arm with both of her hands, trying to pull away apparently. There was no real tugging, just holding onto my arm. Her legs weren't really kicking at all. She was moving around a little, very little. But no sound at all came from her, and at that time I thought that she was so embarrassed or so shocked at what had just happened that she really couldn't say anything and that she was waiting for me to make a move. I didn't really think that I had cut her wind off so completely that not even a little squeak or any gasp or anything had come out.

"So I pulled her back farther and looked down into her face, and her eyes were bulging badly. Her face with turning black at that point, and this was moments after I had grabbed her. Her face was turning from a bright red to a black, and I realized that I was actually cutting her wind off completely. Later on I realized I had crushed her larynx or at least dislocated it to where she couldn't breathe. . . . When she went limp completely, I dropped her to the floor and tied the bags around her head with a cord after I had put the tape over her mouth, which really didn't work; so I just pulled that off.

"When she completely quit struggling, there were some automatic reflexes in the lung area. Her chest was heaving once in a while. When that all stopped, I took her into the bedroom, and her belongings—removed all her clothes, put her on my bed in my bedroom, covered her up with a blanket, went into the other room with her belongings, removed the money from her wallet."

For once Kemper's memory failed him, and he was unable to remember precisely how much money was there, but it had been a substantial amount.

He said apologetically, "I had been keeping track of things like that with the other victims, but in this case I was blowing wide open. I just took any money that anybody had. It might have been ten dollars or fifteen, maybe twenty. I don't know. The credit cards—I had already taken some from my mother. I had several gas credit cards and took a couple I didn't have from my mother's pocketbook, which I had placed under the bed out of the way."

He then took Mrs. Hallett's car and drove down to the Jury Room, parking right next to the cars and motorcycles of some of the men who worked in the courthouse offices across the street. In the Jury Room that day, people who knew Big Ed thought he seemed unusually silent and abstracted. Killing time, he drank beer for an hour or so, hoping always to over-hear some comment by a lawman that would indicate how far the investigations had gone.

Returning to the house at 609-A Ord, he found that Mrs. Hallett's body was in rigor mortis. He decided to sever her head and in doing so discovered he had already broken her neck. He left her body on his bed and spent that night on the bed of his slain mother. He told officers he may have gotten only six hours of sleep that night.

Early Easter Sunday morning (Job celebrating the glory of the Resurrection), he transferred Mrs. Hallett's body to a closet and put his entire arsenal into her car.

Describing this to the investigators, Kemper halted and went back to certain details he had forgotten. Getting it all down just so. In killing Mrs. Hallett he had placed the plastic bag on her head and used the cord as a noose to strangle her, placed his foot on her head as he pulled—but air kept getting into the bag, perhaps through a tear, so he had abandoned that strategy. And finally he got out the white woolen muffler taken from Aiko, the one her mother had bought her the previous year, and strangled Mrs. Hallett with it. That, he said, had seemed to do the trick.

But Sergeant Aluffi was not satisfied. Had he sexually assaulted his mother or Mrs. Hallett? Kemper replied only that he had attempted to have intercourse with the latter, the night before fleeing.

"Do you feel," asked Sergeant Aluffi, "that you've got urges to kill people, or is it just something kind of spontaneous?"

"Well, it's kind of hard to go around killing somebody just for the hell of it," Kemper said. "It's not a kicks thing, or I would have ceased doing it a long time ago. It was an urge. I wouldn't say it was on the full of the moon or anything, but I noticed that no matter how horrendous the crime had been or how vicious the treatment of the bodies after death . . . still, at that point in my crimes the urge to do it again coming as often as a week or two weeks afterwards—a strong urge, and the longer I let it go the stronger it got, to where I was taking risks to go out and kill people—risks that normally, according to my little rules of operation, I wouldn't take because they could lead to arrest."

Sergeant Aluffi asked whether he had ever planned to kill people he knew.

"Oh, I did have fantasies about that," Kemper said, "But one of my rules of operation was that I not do something like that unless it was at the last moment and everything was up in the air and there was no chance of keeping it quiet, as in the case of my mother and Mrs. Hallett."

"You mentioned to me at one time," Aluffi prompted, "that you had a fantasy of killing everybody on your block in Aptos."

"Yeah. That was one of my things. I'd feel inadequate there, feel like everybody's catching up with me, and I'm not doing anything. Considering the abilities I did have, in say creating a calm about me where people weren't excited or suspicious or nervous, and had the trust of most of the people around me, I believed and I still believe that had I wanted to, just as a demonstration—and I thought of making this a demonstration to the authorities in Santa Cruz—how serious this was, and how bad a foe they had come up against, or how difficult a one, or how crafty, or whatever—I had thought of annihilating the entire block that I lived on . . . Not only the block that I lived on but the houses approaching it, which could have included as many as ten or twelve families. And it would be a very slow, a very slow, quiet attack, where no one would be aware of what was going on in the surrounding area; and this would have happened very quickly. Of course, I wouldn't have been involved as I was in the other killings. I would have done it and left, I think, very unnoticeably by the other people that would still be there."

Aluffi asked the Confessor to enlarge on his "rules of operation."

"For a long time," Kemper said, pleased by the opportunity, "I just drove around, originally with the purpose of getting to know people more and seeing where people's heads were at (not trying to make a pun) that were my own age or younger, because I had quite a gap of existence there and quite a gap of awareness in my having been to Atascadero, and going through quite a few different programs where my awareness of myself and my surroundings, I do believe, was a little bit more acute than the people I had to live with and deal with out on the streets.

"This is a problem we approached in the hospital," he said, "and solved theoretically, but it was very difficult on the streets to gain an honest rapport with other people who weren't aware of these special problems of an ex-mental patient who didn't want to be known as an ex-mental patient.

"I drove around picking up several people and noticing the different situations—like girls were hitchhiking alone and in pairs and quite naïvely and quite innocently, and people weren't paying any attention, and I could pick up as many people as I wanted—as often as I wanted—without authorities really becoming aware of it. They were about their own duties. Some of them, I suppose, included watching certain characters that had been picking people up where there had been complaints.

"So, rather than think of a rape-type thing . . . threatening the people not to turn you in (I'd been through all that at Atascadero and watched hundreds and hundreds of rapists go through, and always being caught eventually). So I decided to kind of mix the two and have a situation of rape and a murder and no witness and no prosecution."

It was often said that Kemper's killings were random, but insofar as the girls and his mother were concerned, they were only random within a category of likely victims. Little study has been given to the victims of violent crime, probably because in America there is a peculiarly negative feeling toward them, and it is not unusual for those who survive to wind up feeling almost as guilty as the criminal. In fact the spectacular notoriety that usually rewards the criminal, when combined with the weakness of his victims, produces a strong motivating force for violence.

Kemper's rules of operation ought of course to be read by every potential victim, such as, for starters, every female hitch-hiker. But they will not be, primarily because the most salient characteristic of the victim-prone person is the conviction that he or she is watched over and protected by the Sun, the Moon, the Wind Goddess, and St. Christopher; and, in short, that it could never happen to him or to her.

Kemper also attempted to explain to Sergeant Aluffi the social motivations of his acts, but he must have known that these were only partially true and that the real causes lay deep in the terrifying bogs of his psyche. His sexual reactions and feelings before and after the killings he also described. A sick person makes a poor autodiagnostician, but Kemper with his years of psychoanalysis had greater insight than most. It was always felt that he was holding back the real key to his behavior, and it was suspected that he had also done this with the doctors at Atascadero.

Even when revealing the most shocking of his acts, he derived much pleasure from the impact he was able to make on veterans. The good Sergeant Aluffi made a satisfying audience.

Thus he enlarged on procedures that were designed to baffle and bedazzle the most sagacious detectives:

"My first rule of operation was to be observant of everything around me, far before the approach. If I knew I was going to commit a crime on a certain day, I watched very carefully the situation—the flow of traffic, how heavy the police traffic was, how observant they were being of me in particular and the people around me, the mood of the hitchhikers, which pretty much was according to what day it was. On weekends, everybody was hitchhiking and nobody was paying any attention.

"Sometimes," he said, "there were police and sometimes there weren't. So Rule Number One was to watch the traffic and try not pick anybody up when it's too light or when there are too many people out on foot around the area. These weren't fantastically specific rules. It was more general things.

"From then on I did not pick people up for sport any more. It was for possible execution."

(*Execution* is defined by the dictionary as *capital punishment*. Kemper, by no means incidentally, voted *for* the 1972 California initiative that led to restoration of the death penalty for certain kinds of first degree murder. *Execution* by definition also carries the force of judicial writ by which an officer is empowered to carry a judgment into effect. At this point Kemper as Job changed places with God.)

"I didn't pick up males anymore;" he said, "It was all coeds, and it would only be if they were a possible candidate for death—which would mean that they were young, reasonably good looking, not necessarily well-to-do, but say, of a better class of people than the scroungy, messy, dirty, smelly, hippy types I wasn't at all interested in. I suppose *they* would have been more convenient, but that wasn't my purpose. My little social statement was, I was trying to hurt society where it (would) hurt the worst, and that was by taking its valuable . . . future members of the working society; that was the upper class or the upper-middle class, what I considered to be snobby or snotty brass, or persons that was actually—that ended up later being better equipped to handle a living situation than I was, and be more happily adjusted."

The flaws in the social and political education of this highly intelligent person were abundantly revealed in this statement, not only in the scrambled sense of class structure but in his interpretation of words such as *coed* and *hippy*. Kemper after his long isolation could be forgiven his assumption that *coed* was a perfectly acceptable term for a woman student in the 1970's, since it also sprang readily to the lips of journalists and police, but his violent hatred of hippies was a more complicated matter, perhaps related to long-haired men and his fear of homosexuality. But apparently he could not accept the fact that the hippy he so despised was apt to be a member of the educated upper-middle-class, the often gentle seeker of a way out of the rip-off society, usually with one or more academic degrees, and access to any number of doors. Nor had Kemper understood, which was a great pity, that the doors stood wide open even to an ex-mental patient, provided he was white, bright, and male. Walking through these doors, however, required an ego, and his for years had been a basket case.

He explained to Sergeant Aluffi how things looked to him.

"I consider it a very phony society, a very phony world, where people are too busy copping out to so many things to exist and fit into a group that they had lost sight of their individual aims and goals. I had become completely lost, and very bitter about what I considered these phony values and phony existence, and decided I was going, not necessarily to weed things out—because I would have ended up killing most of the world if I weeded out—but I was striking out at what was hurting me the worst, which was the area, I guess, deep down, I wanted to fit in the most, and I had never fit in, and that was the in-group."

But he had not finished with describing his rules of operation and reverted to them.

"One was, I would not circle back if I saw a good prospect. I would not circle back to pick her up unless I was really out on a limb and I hadn't run in to anybody all week. There was a couple of exceptions to the rule, like the first killings. I had turned around a couple of blocks up, but I realized then I was really sticking my neck out and being obvious to several people. I was quite lucky nobody noticed . . . but I did turn around and go back and pick up those girls. So to be inconspicuous was the order of the day.

"I had no wild things on my car, no wild clothes, no flashy driving. It was strictly down the line, very casual, very relaxed. Smiling only when I approached the girls, because to sit around smiling a lot in the car would draw notice every now and then. I wanted to be absolutely nondescript. Being six-foot-nine inches, it's difficult."

So Edmund Kemper scrunched down in the seat. He always had prospective routes in mind on which to take his victims, and excuses for going there, and he would not threaten them until he was sure no one was in the immediate area.

"I also locked the door from the inside by placing the broken window-turning knob from my side of the car into the opening mechanism on the passenger side, which was not visible from inside the car. And I would open the door on the inside for these people, then place the knob in after they'd get in . . . I would never produce a weapon until I was sure that from then on I had it pretty well licked, the whole situation.

"From that point on I would take absolutely no chances if I didn't have to, which unfortunately was kind of ego-demanding, because I would love to have been the big bad effective rapist or the effective male-ego type, where I could be in control of the situation without a weapon. I usually put the weapon away but let them know it was right there . . . They would never know they were gonna die until they were under attack physically . . ."

Rape, in case Sergeant Aluffi had not yet grasped that important fact, was "just way too chancy."

"Sometimes sex was committed either during the death or after, but there were no sexual attacks . . . before unconsciousness was achieved in any of the cases."

Aluffi asked if he had been taking drugs.

"No," Kemper said. "I was not under any outside things, chemical or physical. I was legally sober every time. I got drunk quite often afterwards; sometimes I was drunk before. But when I would go out looking for some victim to kill, I was always sober or legally sober. I wouldn't feel the influence. I never took any drugs at all."

Aluffi asked how he felt about his mental abilities at the time of the killings.

"How do you mean that? You mean, mental stability—my mental scope, the way I view the world, my mental reactions?"

"Yeah," the sergeant said. "Well, your reactions, your mental stability. Do you feel that—?"

"I feel personally I was quite insane at the time I was committing the crimes," Kemper said. "I felt fearful before I would commit the crimes. But when I'm actually beginning to get myself involved in a crime, it was a big thrill. It was a very strong sensual, sexual excitement, and in some ways it replaced the sexual drive, let's say; but there was always a disappointment in not achieving a sexual rapport, let's say, with the victim. That's why the sex after death sometimes, because it's through frustration."

Aluffi asked if he had had any kind of "sexual achievement" while killing his victims.

"Yes," Kemper said, "I'm sure it's happened before, but the only time I actually noticed an ejaculation was as I was killing Mrs. Hallett on Saturday night. As she was dying, it was a great physical effort on my part, very restraining, very difficult. . . . I went into a full complete physical spasm. . . . I just completely put myself out on it, and as she died, I felt myself reaching orgasm. In the other cases, the physical effort was less."

Aluffi questioned him about why he dissected the bodies and beheaded them.

"Originally," Kemper said, "the decapitations, I think part of it was kind of a weird thing I had in my head. It was a fantasy I had had in childhood. I don't know where it came from, but it was always something I had wanted to do. And it did facilitate part of my plan later; that is, if someone was found they would be harder to identify . . .

"But there was satisfaction gained in the removal of the head. In fact, the first head I ever removed was that of Anita in the trunk of the car with the knife that killed Mary Ann, and I remember it was very exciting, removing Anita's head. There was actually a sexual thrill. And, in fact, there was almost a climax to it. It was kind of an exalted, triumphant-type thing, like taking the head of a deer or an elk or something would be to a hunter."

Aluffi expressed curiosity about the different time intervals that separated Kemper's killings.

"Part of it was fear," the killer said. "Some of it was regret. Other parts of it were the opportunities. I didn't just rush out and look for the opportunities. If you will notice, there was a greater time span between the first and second, and the second and third, than there was anywhere else. But I had started to really get into gear towards the end there. I was getting what I think is sicker, and it was much more of a need for more of the blood—and the blood got in my way. It wasn't something I desired to see. Blood was an actual pain in the ass. What I wanted to see was the *death,* and I wanted to see the *triumph,* the *exultation over the death.* It was like eating, or a narcotic, something that drove me more and more and more."

He explained that when he had the .22 revolver; it facilitated the "quickening." It stepped everything up, "made it much simpler, much easier, much quicker, less of a threat to me personally. I was less afraid to attack. I didn't like attacking people. My whole thing was that if I had been obsessed by attacking people, I would have been in bar fights and street fights, and would have been physically and verbally assaulted. There I wasn't.

"It was a matter of—I didn't care how I got there. I just wanted the exultation over the other party. In other words, winning over death. They were dead and I was alive. That was a victory in my case.

"I suppose I could have been doing this with men, but that always posed more of a threat. They weren't nearly as vulnerable. And that would have been quite odd and probably noticeable, picking up other men and having killed them. Plus, like in the case where sex is involved, or the thrill of having a woman around, alive and dead, wasn't there with a man. So, like I said, there was a threat of the possible retaliation or the possible defense that would throw me off, and after I had broken my arm this was absolutely unthinkable.

"So it wasn't just deaths I wanted. It was, like I said, somewhat of a social statement in there too, and I was jumping upon—I could have gotten children, I suppose. Children are vulnerable. But there are two things against that. One is the most important—that is that children are innocent.

"Children are unknowing. And I have always been very protective of children for that reason. I was very sensitive as a child about the treatment I got and the treatment other children got. And these girls weren't much more than children, I suppose, but I felt—excepting the Aiko case—I felt that they were old enough to know better than to do the things they were doing and . . . out there hitchhiking, when they had no reason or need to. They were flaunting in my face the fact that they could do any damn thing they wanted, and that society is as screwed up as it is. So that wasn't a prime reason for them being dead. It was just something that would get me a little uptight, the thought of that, the feeling so safe in a society where *I* didn't even feel safe."

Even with his sense of irony, Kemper did not perceive the *Catch-22* in his reasoning but could rail at girls for venturing into a dangerous jungle when he was the reason the jungle was dangerous. Yet he knew there were other killers at large, competitors of his like Mullin, and plenty more. And even he did not feel safe with himself, considering he had voted to reinstate the death penalty and later, in jail, would twice attempt suicide. But mainly the voice that spoke was Job's, blaming the women for "flaunting" because *he* had these crazy sex drives; it was his authoritative forebears speaking out, asserting the male's absolute right to invoke punishment upon the female for being female.

Under Aluffi's patient questioning, he disclosed many of the most revolting details of disfiguring the dissected heads: the removal of teeth to prevent dental chart comparisons, the preservation of bits of skin and hair, which like his grisly Polaroid pictures, became keepsakes. The heads themselves he sometimes kept until decay set in.

Although he insisted that he had killed only six students, he disclosed that many more had had close shaves. He told for example, of picking up a girl in Santa Rosa, in another college-campus area north of San Francisco.

"There was almost a victim there, but I guess pretty much for the same reason I didn't kill so many others—it was a surprise pickup and quite a lovely young lady, and I just psychologically was not prepared for it. But when I was psychologically in the mood for it and everything worked out right, the person didn't have a chance when I knew ahead of time."

The Santa Rosa girl, who was sixteen or seventeen years of age, he had deposited safely.

"What about Los Angeles?" Aluffi asked.

"No. I picked people up down there for the same reason only on one occasion—two girls—and I released them at their destination; and picked up one girl in Santa Barbara who was headed for Santa Cruz. But at that time all I had was my knife, and I really didn't see an opportunity to use it."

When Aluffi asked whether he had ever picked up girls in Las Vegas, he insisted that he had not, but in his forthcoming way said, "I would love to take credit for more, not because I am looking for a big score, but—I wouldn't take credit for any that I didn't do, because, well, there's particularly the guilt factor involved, and there is also the—well, I didn't do it, so I didn't get any pleasure out of it or any guilt out of it, and why take somebody off the hook who did it?

"Obviously, whoever did these other crimes that haven't been solved doesn't have too many clues against him. I am not trying to pat anybody on the back or help anybody else get away with anything—but I figure I can't even cop out to these crimes, because they are going to find out that I didn't do them, and I wouldn't be able to give you any details, not even under a lie detector test."

The idea, that in confessing to murders he had not committed Kemper might also have left other killers free to take more lives, did not appear in his reasoning as a valid point favoring the truth. But ingrained rah-rah U.S. "sportsmanship" and the disgrace of claiming a score he had not earned, loomed large. And the other side of *that* coin was, "Screw Herbie Mullin."

He told Aluffi that he would be willing to submit to a lie detector test, so long as it only pertained to cases.

"You know, there's always questions people don't like to sit there and have a lie detector test on concerning other parts in their lives." But he was willing to submit to the test on "any unsolved murders that you might think I had something to do with, or to verify certain statements I have made concerning the crimes I did commit."

His aversion to "fishing expeditions" indicated that, in his own mind at least, he had some shame that transcended multiple murder, mutilation, and necrophilia. Did this have to do with the cooking and eating of human flesh that he confessed to later, or was it again his fear of homosexuality? Was it the final act with his mother that he thought might never come out? Or was it a memory from so far back in childhood that he could not be sure it had ever occurred?

When Aluffi sought again for Kemper's affirmation that all his statements had been made freely and without coercion, promises, or threats, he said, "Maybe it should not be on the record . . . but I am of the view that . . . this whole process is merely a matter to decide by which method I won't see society again. And I certainly wouldn't trust me in society again. So, not having any promises or threats facing me—I mean, who could threaten me? I could be threatened with death, decapitation; someone could threaten to even eat me."

An attorney could have cited this as evidence that Kemper was somewhat muddled as to whether he was or was not confessing under threat or at least that his thoughts at the time were less lucid, but there is no record that the point was ever raised. His eagerness to confess was demonstrated too often and with too much evidence of clarity elsewhere.

Between the preliminary confessions in Colorado and subsequent voluntary additions to the record in Alameda and Santa Cruz counties upon his return to California, he obligingly directed officers to the many locations at which he had disposed of bodies and parts of bodies. This took several days.

But after the many months in which his secrets had been kept locked up inside him and his fearful weariness as a "walking time bomb," this new security of a barred cell and the importance of an official ear were overwhelming. It seemed that he could not stop explaining.

"The important things," he told Sergeant Aluffi, "basically, what happened before and after the crimes, whether anybody suffered, and how much—well, who can say? Basically, when I am thinking back on the crimes, the first three did suffer to an extent; not deliberately, not intentionally. But the last did not suffer, very definitely, and if I had not disposed of that .22 pistol, that would have been the method of death, and it would have gotten down to a certain level of efficiency.

"I would have maintained that as my method of death, and I am actually quite glad I did get rid of that pistol, because I would have been terribly tempted to use it in my travels in the last days of my freedom. Any other method with the other weapons would have been quite difficult and very hazardous. But I did intend when I took these weapons with me not to hide in the corner and defend myself. But I hadn't planned to make a last great outburst. But towards the end there, I started feeling the folly of the whole damn thing, and at the point of near exhaustion, near collapse, I just said the hell with it and called it all off. I couldn't so much worry about myself getting killed or hurt. I just didn't want to see anybody else get hurt or killed trying to stop me from what I had been doing."

Law enforcement officers, as mentioned earlier, did not accept this explanation wholeheartedly, believing that Kemper's long-distance surrender was motivated mainly by self-interest and his fear of physical harm.

Aluffi was curious as to just why Kemper wanted to tell his "complete story." Kemper replied that it was only *mostly* a complete story.

"But my main purpose," he said, "is getting it off my chest, because whatever is on my chest must stay, I am sure, but let's say I had some Accounts Payable and I closed my Accounts Receivable, and so I had to balance the accounts. I guess I could be facetious about it and say, well, I give you guys a year to catch up with me. And I mean, shit, I couldn't keep on going forever . . . I really couldn't have. Emotionally I couldn't handle it much longer.

"So, considering—I don't know who would consider me lucky that I didn't get caught. But considering that I wasn't . . .

I had to do something. I am sure they were trying, but with the tools the police have to work with and with the basic concept that society isn't as cold-blooded and ruthless and back-stabbing as I am, they didn't really have . . . And I was being rather cunning about the whole thing. And . . . it was obvious that I premeditated every crime, just by the fact that I didn't get caught on any of them.

"There's no way that odds or luck or anything else could have had anything to do with getting away with that many crimes. And if I had kept my mouth shut, I would have gotten away with them, I think, forever. But I knew I wouldn't stop, and I didn't really want to go out and kill all the young coeds in the world. I wouldn't have. I am sure measures would have kept me from doing that. But I hadn't—as soon as this area . . . dried up, I would have gone to another and do it, and I may have ended up driving a thousand miles to kill two or three people. But by that time, how many would have been dead?"

He was in a philosophical mood. It seemed as if his mind was being unburdened of years, as if he could not have stopped talking—

"It was starting to weigh kind of heavy, so originally my thought was . . . that I would continue forever; but let's say, at the level of the game—let's say I wore out of it, and the original purpose was gone. Let's say I started returning to some lucid moments where I—where I started to burn out the hate and fear, and I guess disappointments of the coeds that were already dead, and the need that I had for continuing death was needless and ridiculous. It wasn't serving any physical or real or emotional purpose. It was just a pure waste of time. How's that?"

Sergeant Aluffi, noncommital, then steered Kemper back to the time of fleeing his mother's house. There were some gaps in that picture. Where had he gone and how?

Kemper was glad he asked because it put his memory for fine detail to work again. Before leaving that house of death he had dressed carefully—in his dress boots, the blue denim bell bottoms that he had worn in most of the killings, a white shirt, and his brown buckskin jacket. The latter was stained on the inside from the first two murders.

At ten o'clock Easter Sunday morning, driving Mrs. Hallett's car, he went directly out of town, heading eastward, refueled in Sacramento, and drove straight through to Reno, Nevada, winding up as if drawn by a magnet on the campus of the University of Nevada. What to do with a car that he feared would soon be the object of an interstate search? First he rented a Hertz car and transferred the guns into it.

He drove the Hallett car to a nearby Texaco station, told the operator the car had electrical problems, and left it—knowing that to check it over could take days. In the rented car he continued driving in an easterly direction, unsure of the highway, feeling mentally confused, stopping only for gas or soft drinks with which to wash down the No-Doz.

After eighteen hours of driving, he was stopped by a highway patrolman in Colorado—for speeding. His carbine was under the blanket in the back seat at the time. Like the lawmen Kemper had encountered in California, the patrolman, deceived by manner and appearances, never thought of examining the car. But he gave Kemper the option of paying a fine of $25.00 in cash or appearing in court.

When Kemper said he would pay, the patrolman accompanied him to the nearest mailbox and deposited $25.00 of his badly needed cash. He was very concerned about the danger of being stopped again, knowing that his description was easily remembered. It seemed likely that an All Points Bulletin had been put out by now. He also feared the FBI might be after him.

In numbed panic, he continued driving toward Eastern Colorado, taking as many as three No-Doz in a half hour, driving far into Monday night. But still he had heard nothing on the radio about the crimes committed in California. And this made him think again of the mutilation of his mother, for the severing of her left hand, he felt sure, would at once tip off the police as to his guilt. It was "symbolic, I suppose."

Of the decapitation, he said, "I wanted to make absolutely

sure there wasn't any suffering. But the hand; I think it is like the left-hand-of-God thing. I had always considered my mother very formidable, very fierce, and very forbidding. She had always been a very big influence on my life, and whether I hated her or loved her, it was very dynamic. And the night she died . . . it was amazing to me how much like every other victim of mine she had died; how vulnerable and how human she was. It shocked me quite some time. I am not sure that it still doesn't shock me."

As one who had always looked up biblical terms he did not understand, he knew that the left hand was God's punishing hand; and who but a guilty and left-handed son would cut off his mother's left hand?

Still, he continued, "I felt quite relieved after her death. A lot of it was guilt that I had been building up and fear that she would find out about what had happened and what it would do to her. I was glad that it had been quick."

He told of passing through the tiny town of Holly, Colorado.

"It was very late at night. I was exhausted. And I was past exhaustion. I was just running on pure adrenaline. My body was quivering at times and my mind was slowly just beginning to unravel. I felt I was losing control, and I was afraid that anything could cause me to go off the deep end, and I didn't know what would happen then. I had never been out of control in my life."

Kemper's seeming inconsistencies about self-control were cleared up when he distinguished between mental and physical control. At times he said that two beings inhabited his body; that it was "kind of like a blacking out;" and, "You know what you're doing but you don't notice anything else around."

But to Sergeant Aluffi he explained: "I had lost control of my body. I experienced this in the killing of my grandparents when I was fifteen. I just completely lost control of myself. But as far as my mind went, I had realized what was going on and I couldn't stop it. In this case my body was just exhausted and my mind was starting to go. I was hallucinating. Not so much seeing things that weren't there, but I was imagining things happening that weren't happening; and normally when I am driving too long, I experience visual hallucinations. In this case it was emotional and mental hallucinations. . . . I was completely wound up.

"I finally had a thought. I was trying to think, 'Wow, I have got to stop this because it is getting so far out of hand. I am not going to be responsible for what happens any further. It is just going to happen,' and I didn't know what it was, and I didn't like that idea. So I came upon the idea of calling up Lieutenant Charles Scherer at the Santa Cruz Police Department, long distance, knowing I couldn't wait until morning. . . . I just wanted to say where I was and see what I could arrange as far as a surrender, and if it was not satisfactory, then I would continue on."

When word of Kemper's surrender reached Santa Cruz, his friends began streaming into the sheriff's department to express their shocked disbelief that the quiet, courteous fellow they knew could be a mass murderer.

The portrait that emerged was a friendly, slow-fused person. "He never focused on violence," a good friend noted. And another claimed that he never picked up hitchhikers.

A drinking crony told of spending part of Saturday night with him at the Jury Room, where they stayed until after midnight. "He seemed a little quieter than usual Saturday night," the man said, but did not seem "upset" about anything.

As word of Kemper's apprehension reached the press, and as he led lawmen on an exhausting round of the various sites of buried fragments of corpses, a group of reporters began to follow. Perversely, this attention angered him. Sometimes he refused to point out the burial sites until the press had been removed. Finally, the giant in leg-irons and manacles led a group of officers to the back yard of his mother's house.

The girl next door, her eyes riveted on the boy next door, watching with other neighbors as a skull was removed from a spot about four feet from the rear of Clarnell Strandberg's house. It was Cynthia's. One neighbor, visibly shaken, said, "To think we've been living here so peacefully with that laying in the ground."

The girl next door shivered and nodded.

The six-foot-nine-inch suspect towered over his seven guards as he stood for arraignment in the Santa Cruz court. He was charged with the slaying of eight persons, including his mother.

CHAPTER FIFTEEN

FOLLY OF M'NAGHTEN RULE

DOWN THE COAST in San Luis Obispo where he was now in private practice, Dr. William J. Schanberger, clinical psychologist, turned on the eleven o'clock news and learned for the first time of Kemper's confessions. He had been director of the psychology laboratory at Atascadero State Hospital during most of the years of Kemper's confinement. It was under him that Kemper had worked so willingly and diligently as a crew leader.

Dr. Schanberger had seen him almost every day during these years, had taken a considerable interest in him, and thought that he knew him well. Dr. Dorothy Pollock, the psychiatrist who treated Kemper during his hospitalization and who could claim to know him even better, had also left the hospital. She was retired and now spent much of her time traveling.

When the full impact of the news hit him, Schanberger said, "I was shocked, devastated. Afterward, I spent several weeks going through phases of reaction about it. I felt numbed, horrified, bewildered, and finally even angry at Kemper for letting everybody down. For weeks it preoccupied my mind.

"You go through a long period of working with somebody and you think you know them, and then some terrible thing happens and you can't figure out what happened, why it all went wrong."

What he and the other doctors at Atascadero found hardest to understand was why Kemper had made no effort to get in touch with them when he felt himself regressing. Perhaps this was naive of them, since Kemper valued his freedom more than he feared himself.

Dr. Frank J. Vanasek, now director of admissions at Patton State Hospital, had been chief of research at Atascadero during Kemper's confinement. He, Schanberger, and several others on the medical staff who had been involved in his treatment—although they were now widely scattered—gathered for a special session at which they sifted Kemper's records and went over everything they could recall about the case, trying to arrive at some understanding of what had gone wrong. Had they simply erred in releasing him prematurely? Had his problems been wrongly diagnosed? Had new stresses occurred on the "outside" that detonated the self-styled "walking time bomb"? One critical factor, of course, was that they had never intended, and had strongly recommended against, his returning to his mother's home.

But the meeting broke up inconclusively. Later, information came out at the trial that caused Dr. Vanasek to entertain second thoughts about the case.

Kemper's shocking regression after his release from Atascadero, combined with the inadvertent complicity of the two Fresno doctors whose testimony was instrumental in sealing his juvenile murder record—coming as they did in the wake of the Mullin case and Mullin's history of release from several mental hospitals—sent public confidence in the forensic psychiatrists and psychologists thudding to a new low. As always, scapegoats were needed.

Their colleagues far and near, understanding the odds, and the risk that doctors in mental hospitals and prisons had to take as a matter of course, rallied somewhat raggedly to the support. The most striking thing for the layman was the discovery that hardly any of the behaviorists could agree, except in their insistence that it was the public that needed educating. *They* had never claimed that the state of the art was perfect. The sooner people accepted the fact of high risk, the better.

One Bay Area psychiatrist said of the two Fresno doctors, "These guys weren't stupid; they were victims of the odds."

Dr. David Marlowe, chairman of the board of studies for psychology at UCSC, who had known Clarnell Strandberg well at the University—Kemper's sister Allyn sometimes babysat for the Marlowe family—agreed with this assessment. Marlowe interviewed Kemper at the public defender's request, but like Schanberger and others, refused to testify for him.

Dr. Herbert McGrew, a staff psychiatrist at Napa State Hospital, said, "Kemper is a marvelous example of the fact that psychiatrists don't know everything. If you're right seventy-five per cent of the time, you're doing pretty well."

But Marlowe, when he heard this, snorted and said, "Just the reverse is true. Out of one hundred persons, we might make a correct prognosis on ten or fifteen."

He explained, "No one can predict behavior because no one can predict the stresses that a person may undergo sometime in the future."

Of schizophrenia, which Mullin and possibly Kemper as a child may have suffered from, he said, "It is quantitative, not qualitative like cancer or tuberculosis. You or I have at some time in our lives shown schizophrenic symptoms. Under stress, we suffer from confusion, blackouts, disorientation. The schizophrenic is not properly equipped with defenses and techniques for handling the stress and tension.

"Psychiatrists should never say a person will not be dangerous.

"The question with no answer," he said, "is *how far society must go for protection*. Must we keep seventy or eighty men in a jail or mental hospital for life because five of them, if released, may turn out to be killers? Where do we draw the line?"

Dr. Marlowe in sum asked, "Should society be prepared to sacrifice the occasional murder victim rather than deprive ninety harmless mental patients out of one hundred of their civil rights and freedom?"

As to closing down mental hospitals and returning patients to their communities, hopefully for treatment, enlightened laymen felt ambivalent about the issue while others found the trend angering and alarming. The community was the place where the patient had become ill to start with. In communities where no local facilities existed, the families were usually unable to cope with the released patient.

Dr. Marlowe pointed out that the halfway houses being developed in some communities were often shocking places. "There's lots of money to be made in this. People have gone out and bought run-down Victorian mansions, for example, in which they house and feed patients, but no one keeps track of how well. Occasionally a psychologist runs through, but it is still just custodial care, the same as in the old-fashioned 'warehouses'—except that now it is in the community and people are making money out of it."

Across the nation the population of state mental institutions had declined by almost one-half between 1963 and 1972. The Community Mental Health Centers Act passed in 1963 was intended to eliminate the "human warehouses" by creating 2,000 local clinics to provide counseling and care.

The state hospitals began discharging their patients as planned, but with money to fund the local centers provided only in driblets, the revolution faltered. A decade later, only 392 community centers were in operation. Especially in large states such as New York and California, the number of patients far exceeded the ability of the communities to treat them.

The Nixon administration in 1973 announced plans to phase out the federal grants that had served as matching funds for the centers, and then tried to impound funds already appropriated by Congress. The National Council of Community Mental Health Centers sued and won its money—which, however, still fell far short of the budgetary need.

An investigation by the Long Island newspaper, *Newsday*, disclosed that patients released from the state hospitals in New York often were jammed into "tiny rooms, basements, and garages and fed a semi-starvation diet of rice and chicken necks . . . by operators who . . . confiscate their monthly welfare checks."

In California the controversy over closure of state hospitals reached a climax in 1974. In the space of a mere two years, *seventy-four* persons had been killed by patients released from such institutions.

The Reagan administration, notoriously more concerned for penny-pinching than for humane medical care (ironically, while trumpeting for law-and-order), sought through the governor's veto to retain the final authority as to whether California's remaining eleven state hospitals should be closed. The legislature, motivated by angry and fearful voters, overrode the veto. This, of course, did not mean that mental health care at the community level would be improved, but it did indicate a go-slow policy on closing the state hospitals.

Dr. Abe Linn, the administrator of Napa State Hospital, urged that one state hospital be kept open for northern California and one for the south.

"It's possible," he said, "for the community to take care of any patients, mentally ill or mentally retarded, if the taxpayers are willing to pay the very expensive costs."

San Francisco, for example, is able to provide good community mental health service, but many smaller California cities and towns cannot afford to.

Some of the older huge state hospitals have been converted recently to serve more than one type of need, as for example, Patton State Hospital near San Bernardino, one of whose new roles is to share with Atascadero the treatment of the mentally ill sex offender who has been convicted of a crime and is on an indeterminate commitment. But it has several new functions.

Patton, as one of the prototypes, had an original population of nine thousand patients, the more able of whom helped to run the hospital farm and maintain the grounds and its outstanding arboretum. In the old days, patients took care of a herd of prize cattle. In summer they canned fruits and vegetables from the institutional garden. But it was nevertheless a warehouse where the mentally ill tended to collect and never return to society, unless they were fortunate.

Since 1973 Patton has been accepting what are known as "penal code patients"—persons accused of criminal offenses who are too mentally disturbed to stand trial. At Patton they are treated until they are able to understand the charges against them and can take part in their own defense, the law requiring that as soon as medically possible they must stand trial. The court then determines the next step for them. Patton also accepts persons who have been convicted of crimes and found Not Guilty by Reason of Insanity, and who are presently insane. They are treated until they are considered sane or until the hospital decides it cannot predict that they will become sane.

The third type of patient usually consists of men involved in aggressive rape where there has been a *pattern* of maladjustment. But sex criminals judged insane, if they require maximum security, still must be sent to Atascadero State Hospital.

And there is a fourth category of patients at the "new" Patton —the mentally retarded, of whom there are now three hundred.

Among the "penal code patients" are all of California's women offenders who are mentally disturbed—which is a very small group, compared to the number of male patients.

In all, the new Patton State Hospital has six hundred patients, soon to be increased to eight hundred. Its male population is drawn only from the southern portion of the state.

In the near future, however, Patton will again be accepting mentally ill people who have *no* penal records—patients from the community mental health clinics, where they can be held for only seventy-two hours for observation. They will then be sent to Patton for fourteen days, during which time they will be treated and returned home or, if need be, committed for a longer period.

The administration of a hospital serving so many needs undoubtedly will prove complex and difficult—but it may become a necessary pattern for the future in other states sharing California's problems. Research records are kept on every patient, even after they leave.

"We always know," Dr. Vanasek told me, "if a patient has reoffended, or has applied for a gun permit. We keep a rap sheet on everyone."

Whether an application for a gun permit is reported quickly enough, however, is unfortunately another matter.

Vanasek adds, "The criterion of a successful treatment program is follow-up in the community after the patient's release."

At present one in every four who are released come back— or a recidivism rate of twenty-five percent.

killer of Kemper's type, smart and determined, knowing the right answers to the questions (he was said to have memorized the desirable answers to twenty-eight different tests while at Atascadero and claimed that he had himself helped develop a new scale for the testing of overt hostility), will always find a way to get out of a mental institution and to get some kind of weapon, if it is only a knife. But, on his own word, his enthusiasm for murder was greatly reinforced when he was able to buy a new handgun. The outlawing of civilian arsenals, including those of members of the National Rifle Association, and strict enforcement, could be extremely effective in slowing down a Kemper. *Halfway* attempts at gun control, however, will never save his victims.

In the furor that followed Kemper's arrest, Napa's Dr. McGrew pointed to some of the problems that an institutional doctor confronts. For example, psychological tests such as the Rorschach help little in predicting a killer.

He said that he frequently got test results showing a mental patient to be full of hostility and aggression. This type of patient, when released, however, might go back to college and lead a perfectly normal life. The hostility and aggression would still be potentialities. Under certain circumstances, they might erupt again. But no one could say when.

Dr. Bernard Diamond, an outstanding forensic authority—both a psychiatrist and a lawyer—at the University of California, Berkeley, insisted that any clever patient could fool the experts. One had only to learn how to lie or to restrict his responses to the tests.

Dr. Diamond was critical of some of his colleagues who were willing to slant their services to obtain whatever verdict a defense attorney or a prosecutor was out to win. One psychiatrist in California's East Bay, who was reported to make himself available to the authorities day or night, claimed that he could spot a mentally ill person just by looking at him.

Currently the American Academy for Psychiatry and the Law, which Diamond founded, is trying to raise the standards for such "expert" services, but he said there was at present no way to prevent an irresponsible psychiatrist testifying to accommodate the side that hired him.

The man appointed to take the lead in Kemper's defense, James Jackson, the chief assistant public defender for Santa Cruz County, explodes at the mere mention of the word *expert* in conjunction with such forensic witnesses.

"There *are* no experts!" he insists. "They don't know *anything* and most of them are *crazy*."

When I talked with Jackson, he had just defended three mass murderers in a row. A flamboyant man with wild reddish hair, who looks somewhat like a youngish Einstein, his big hands always in motion as he speaks, Jackson seethes with contempt not only for the behavioral scientists but for their whole lexicon of medical labeling.

"These terms are all meaningless in my opinion. What, for example, is the difference between a *sociopathic person* and a *dissocial type?*"

"I'll bite," I said. "I've never heard of the latter."

"Well, *he's* someone who maybe kills ten people and robs a bank on the side. It means *nothing*."

Oddly enough, Jackson's contempt for the jargon was shared by Dr. Joel Fort, with whom he tangled most angrily during the trial.

It was good that Jackson was a man of vast if explosive energy, for the task that lay ahead in defending Edmund Kemper was unenviable in the extreme. Everything went against the defense—primarily the defendant. Not only had Kemper handed the case to the DA on a platter but Jackson was unable to persuade a single psychiatrist or psychologist to take the stand in the defendant's behalf.

Pleas were entered of Not Guilty and Not Guilty by Reason of Insanity.

It did not matter that Kemper had been found insane after killing his grandparents; society would have to find him sane after he had killed eight more times. For only by finding him sane could he be put out of circulation for keeps, punished in a prison rather than treated in a hospital.

Jackson found *one* psychiatrist who would have testified in Kemper's behalf under the "product" rule (Is this crime the *product* of a *diseased mind?*)—but in California only the M'Naghten Rule is admissible. (Did you dig what you did?) And Kemper had left little doubt that he dug.

Harold Cartwright, a young private investigator for the public defender's office and a former policeman—he is now studying law—asked one psychiatrist, who refused to testify that Kemper was legally insane, to answer off-the-record, "Where would you rate him on a scale of one to one hundred—if one hundred was crazy?"

And the psychiatrist said candidly, "Oh, around 275."

Jackson had also defended Frazier and Mullin. They too were adjudged sane, because people were afraid that they would be released and start killing all over again if sent to mental hospitals.

From the moment Kemper was jailed, he began ingratiating himself with his guards and other lawmen, while ridiculing his neighboring cellmate, Herbie Mullin.

A member of the DA's staff said later, "He would be my all-time choice for 'most interesting criminal,' and I've seen a lot of them in twenty years.

"For example, after the jury's verdict, he came forward to the DA at the prosecution table, extended his hand, and said, 'I want to thank you for the restraint you showed throughout this trial.' It's hard to say, 'This guy is a real asshole,' because you don't get that picture talking to him. He is outgoing, friendly, relates well. You have a tendency to forget, talking to him that way, the six young girls, the mother and her friend brutally mutilated. But you also have the feeling that he is not going to bother *you*."

Why did Kemper, when confined adjacent to Herbie Mullin's cell in the San Mateo County Jail, throw water on Mullin? The question was put by a reporter.

"Well, he had a habit of singing and bothering people," Kemper said, "when somebody tried to watch TV. So I threw water on him to shut him up. Then, when he was a good boy, I'd give him peanuts. Herbie liked peanuts. That was effective, because pretty soon he asked permission to sing. That's called behavior modification treatment."

Even Jackson and Harold Cartwright agreed that Mullin's singing voice was dreadful.

Kemper was asked of his cell neighbor whether he thought Mullin to be insane.

"Yes," he said. "Judging from my years in Atascadero, I would say he is mentally ill."

Jackson and Cartwright spent hours and hours questioning Kemper in jail before the trial, trying to unearth evidence of legal insanity or anything else that could help in the defense.

The best potential witness on insanity was Kemper's younger sister Allyn, who until now had kept to herself recollections of many of the bizarre acts and fantasies of her brother's childhood.

Jackson and Cartwright located her, brought her to town, and secretly installed her in a motel the day before the trial started. But that evening Allyn, who herself had had some very close shaves at Edmund's instigation, pondered the nightmare of all that had happened and began to worry about her role. And perhaps very wisely, if impulsively, she telephoned the district attorney, who whisked her off to his house where she spoke for two hours, telling all the important things she could remember about her brother and his lifelong affair with knives and guns.

Jackson said that when he and Cartwright talked with Kemper, he always started giving *them* the Minnesota Multiphasic Personality Inventory. And he never at any time, in Jackson's opinion, told the whole truth.

He fooled his interrogators by always starting to talk about dismemberment, which riveted their attention.

"But we always felt he was holding something back," Jackson said. "The last couple days of the trial, one of his friends gave him a lot of tranquilizers and he began to tell the truth."

But what it was he concealed, the trial experts did not learn. Dr. Frank Vanasek may have come closest to the truth later with his hypothesis.

CHAPTER SIXTEEN

SANE

KEMPER WAS BROUGHT to trial wearing leg-irons and heavily guarded "for his own protection" before Santa Cruz Superior Court Judge Harry F. Brauer.

Wearing his buckskin jacket with the Junior Chamber of Commerce pin in the lapel, he sat listening alertly as a jury was selected. The judge asked that the jurors' names be kept secret to protect them from possible community harrassment, as had occurred during the recent Mullin trial. Since his arraignment in May, the defendant had made one suicide attempt or apparent attempt, trying to cut his wrist veins in jail.

In quick succession he lost the first two rounds of the trial, claiming belatedly that he had wanted to speak to an attorney shortly after his apprehension in Colorado during his first interview.

"I was afraid I might be getting in over my head," he said,

adding that he had so indicated to Lieutenant Scherer.

Judge Brauer, pointing out that Kemper had then immediately gone on to make a most incriminating statement, while "the interviewing officer couldn't even say two words," and that he had twice signed the *Miranda* form as to understanding his full rights, ruled against the motion.

Kemper's elaborate confession, the judge said lyrically, "was not the fruit of a poison tree."

Public Defender Jackson lost a second time trying to have the evidence dismissed, on the ground that Kemper ought to have been returned directly to California and arraigned rather than being driven around for several days pointing out fragments of corpses to the investigators.

But Judge Brauer stated, "California law makes it clear that (such a delay) does not automatically invalidate statements of the defendant."

As the prosecution began playing Kemper's confession, the defendant's voice reciting explicit detail, an air of tension gripped the courtroom. Spectators sat rigidly, some with their mouths agape, and some wept silently.

Families and friends of the victims heard Kemper describe dissections and beheadings, the planning of yet more murders, the buying of weapons, stabbing, shooting, burials. (The defendant had asked to be absent from the courtroom while the tapes were played, but the request was denied by Judge Brauer.)

In the audience, a woman moved her finger across her throat in a slashing motion while staring at Kemper. He became agitated. James Jackson quickly asked Judge Brauer for a recess.

The following morning crowds waited as much as an hour to be admitted into the courtroom, and the judge expressed disgust at the number of teenage girls who packed the spectator section. At one point he asked the bailiff to remove several people, saying the courtroom was too crowded.

Kemper appeared in his orange prison jumpsuit, still in shackles.

The state introduced the note (of a compulsive perfectionist) that he had left in his mother's house after murdering her and Mrs. Hallett:

"Appx. 5:15 A.M. Saturday. No need for her to suffer any more at the hands of this horrible 'murderous Butcher.' It was quick—asleep—the way I wanted it.

"Not sloppy and incomplete, gents. Just a 'lack of time.' I got things to do! ! !"

A detective described finding large puddles of dried blood under the rear seat and in the trunk of the hard-driven, yellow Ford Galaxie. And the tapes played on. Three psychiatrists testified that they had examined Kemper and found him sane.

On Monday October 29 the defendant appeared in court with his wrist heavily bandaged. The day before in his cell he had again attempted suicide, using the ballpoint pen given to him by a journalist to open his veins. Then he had resisted efforts of the guards to help him and had had to be handcuffed before they could get him into an ambulance and take him to a hospital, where six stitches were taken to close the wound. On his return to jail, closed circuit TV had been focused on his cell.

During Monday's hearing Kemper appeared tired and at one point lowered his head to the counsel table and briefly closed his eyes.

In that day's Santa Cruz *Sentinel*, two articles appeared on page one parallel to the trial report. Chancellor Dean McHenry of UCSC announced that the unprecedented wave of murders in the area had caused enrollments at the prestigious university to fall short by at least a hundred students that semester.

And the assistant district attorney confirmed that "forcible rape has become commonplace here."

He and local police detectives, he said, viewed it as the most serious crime after murder. The FBI had reported that an estimated seventy-five per cent of all rapes went unreported by victims out of fear of the stigma attached. The inference was that the law was now prepared to regard such complaints seriously.

The defendant's sister Allyn, who was married and asked to be identified only by her first name, testified that she had had suspicions about her brother's involvement in the slayings for a long time.

When the death and dismemberment of Cynthia were reported, a childhood incident "flashed in front of my face"—the killing and beheading of the family cat.

She had then asked her brother if he had anything to do with the killings and he had denied it, saying, however, "Don't mention this to Mom because she'll start wondering, and I don't want things to get heavy." He told Allyn that Clarnell had already questioned him about the girls' deaths.

Allyn told of visiting her mother's house shortly before Edmund's arrest, at which time, she said, he owned five rifles and one pistol. She spoke of his pride in his arsenal and of her own grave misdoubts. "I was not interested at all in seeing them because of his past."

Only three months before her mother's murder, Allyn had been invited by Edmund to come into his bedroom and see the guns. As she entered the room, he had pulled out a pair of handcuffs and placed them around her wrists.

"I didn't like that," she said, "I said to take them off now."

On the first day of November, Kemper, shaken and distraught, took the stand in his own behalf.

"I wanted the girls for myself—as possessions," he said. "They were going to be mine; they are mine."

He added, "I believe . . . that there are two people inside me." At times it seemed to him that the killings were "horrendous," yet at other times "those feelings don't enter my mind."

He testified that the killings were the result of fantasies that began to build up in him while he was a teenage patient at Atascadero—at the very time, incidentally, when his doctors thought he was making excellent progress.

Under questioning by Jackson, he said he had confessed so freely, "Because I want help. If I go to a penitentiary, I'll be locked up in a little room where I can't hurt anybody and I'll be left to my fantasies." Otherwise, "Someday, somebody will be hurt."

Speaking hesitantly, he affirmed the existence of fantasies as an important part of his life since a very early age. They included the fancied killing and dismembering of many people, including the district attorney and the chief of the Drug Abuse Preventive Center. He had also thought of sniping at anyone who came along.

At times as he spoke, Kemper appeared to be near tears, and occasionally he asked Judge Brauer for a few minutes to collect his thoughts.

"It's kind of hard getting into my fantasy world—it's been private for so long."

Under direct examination by his attorney, he said he had been lying when he had claimed killing the hitchhiking women because they belonged to a social class he resented. In fact, he insisted, he had killed them simply because he wanted them as possessions. His line of "reasoning" was that, "when the girls were alive, they were distant and not sharing with me. I was trying to establish a relationship."

Jackson, trying his best to establish insanity, asked why he had finally disposed of their bodies. The defendant, doing his best to accommodate, replied, "They were rotting—I was losing them."

He had visited their graves often. In the case of Cynthia's head buried in the back yard at his mother's house, he had placed it so that her face was turned toward his bedroom. "I talked to it. I said affectionate things . . . like you would say to a girl friend or a wife."

When Jackson asked why he had slashed his wrists, he said, "I wanted to die—slowly enough to think about what I have done."

For the jury he traced his fantasy world back to as early as the age of four, when he had dreamed of "a mother and father loving and being together and caring for their children."

But the facts as he told them were different: violence, hatred, and yelling between the two huge parents with enormous voices. Once, he claimed, his mother taunted his father until he slammed her against the piano, knowing that he would not strike her. The fact that blows were never struck actually disqualified Kemper's parents from proper standing in the annals of U.S. domestic violence.

In court he painted a grim picture of life at Atascadero and rampant homosexuality among the patients, although at other times it had appeared that his confinement was one of the better periods of his life. For his own part, during that time, he claimed, he had spent a lot of time daydreaming about women. At first he just thought about petting, caressing, and kissing. But after a time, "my fantasies went haywire and started getting violent."

Dr. Joel Fort, a respected Bay Area psychiatrist and a lecturer on sexual deviation and crime at University of California campuses, testified as a court-appointed witness. More than most of his colleagues, Fort had worked directly with the problems of petty criminals, drug addicts, and other "street people."

One reason Dr. Fort was in demand as a prosecution witness in cases of this type was that he had served in the sixties on the California Commission to review and evaluate the state law defining insanity—essentially, the M'Naghten Rule. As it stands today, a person knowing the difference between right and wrong or understanding the nature and quality of his act when wrongfully taking the life of a human being is legally sane. (In this writer's opinion the disparity between medical and legal definitions of insanity perpetuate a fiction that is bizarre and actually harmful, however soothing to some members of the public.)

Fort was asked by the prosecution during Kemper's case, "So a person could be medically diagnosed as a psychotic and schizophrenic and still be legally sane?" And he replied, Definitely, and most commonly that would be the situation."

Opponents of M'Naghten have long held that a defendant would have to be foaming at the mouth to be found Not Guilty by Reason of Insanity—but today even that evidence would not be accepted, for some expert would be found to explain excessive salivation as quite proper considering the times. Even so, the *Oxford English Dictionary* defines *Insane* (from the Latin in 1560) as "Not of sound mind, mad, mentally deranged." In 1842, *Insane actions* were defined as "mad, idiotic, and irrational," and this was in Queen Victoria's reign when the M'Naghten Rule originated.

Fort—with his rub-off from radical students—first of all was determined to establish the fact that *he* was not the sort of psychiatrist who sat around a private office applying Freudian-oriented therapy to pampered neurotics like so many of his colleagues. The latter, he insisted, were mainly concerned with "affluent, middle-class, middle-aged, white women, generally with conditions that are called neuroses; and rarely with conditions that relate to problems such as crime or people from lower socioeconomic groups, or people who cannot regularly make appointments, or live a different kind of life-style."

Defender Jackson, cognizant of two or three white, middle-class, middle-aged women on the jury, prepared himself to pounce as soon as Fort left an opening—which was quite a time in coming.

Fort declared that the other most common kind of practice his colleagues engaged in was working part- or full-time with what are called "community mental health programs." ("That's the modern, accepted terminology for programs that used to simply be called mental hygiene clinics or mental health clinics.") By building up such facilities, he explained, it had been hoped to extend psychiatric care to social rejects who ordinarily failed to get such help, but the catch had been that so many psychiatrists now spent so much of their time doing administrative work that they rarely gave direct help to patients.

He pointed to a third kind of (presumably wayward) psychiatrist who works in state mental hospitals and prisons. Such institutions seek primarily "specialists in administration and, of course, there is some question about whether a medical degree per se makes one a born or skillful leader or administrator, but this is the characteristic practice of those in state hospitals, and most of the work in these institutions is done by lower-paid, less-trained individuals . . . They are called psychiatric technicians and used to be called ward aides . . ."

Determined to leave no dodge undisclosed, Dr. Fort mentioned a fourth kind of expert, who engaged in "academic psychiatry," which was in part his own dodge.

Jackson, unable to restrain his boundless outrage any longer, intervened: "Don't middle-class, neurotic women need love too?"

"Definitely, and hopefully they receive it regularly—"

"That's all."

"But," added Fort, "they don't need it from psychiatrists, necessarily."

Fort then disclosed part of the reason for Jackson's antipathy. The latter had originally asked the doctor to examine Kemper and to conduct an interview of him under sodium amytal or so-called truth serum. Fort had declined but had accepted appointment by Judge Brauer as a court witness, saying, "It seemed to me my major contribution would . . . be to try to serve both sides, and be as independent as possible . . ."

He had spent many hours questioning Kemper and reading his records, which included reports from Atascadero and earlier, as well as his confessions. Fort had also listened to taped interviews conducted by two psychiatrists employed by the public defender, in which Kemper was questioned under truth serum.

He had concluded a number of things about Kemper's mental state, "but the two central themes were an overwhelming sexual curiosity and obsession with sex, to such an extent that, insofar as we use lay language or concepts that have been widely circulated in society, I think he could best be described as a sex maniac, certainly to a greater degree than anyone else I have seen in working with sexual and criminal problems in the past twenty years.

"The second theme," Dr. Fort continued, "was a tremendous range of hatred, rage, or aggressiveness that stemmed from a series of childhood experiences and subsequent experiences, and that involved or included getting back at a society that he felt wronged him, getting back at his mother and father that he felt had wronged him, and in general, the explosive expression of hatred. . . ."

As to the six young women victims, apart from the other

four, "his motives were to have as wide a range of sexual satisfaction and sexual enjoyment or pleasure as he could possibly
have. He felt for reasons perhaps that I will have . . . time later
to explain—he felt inadequate sexually. He felt that he was not
able to have even sexual conversations, let alone any kind of
sexual contact or intercourse with women when they were
alive.

"He had only one sexual encounter, including intercourse,
with a live woman in his history; and she subsequently rejected
him when he approached her for a second time. Feeling unable
to do that, also feeling inadequate about the size of his penis
and about other aspects of his physique, he engaged or began
his sexual pleasure with these young women by his thoughts
about picking them up as hitchhikers, having them in his
power; in other words, moving from the general to the more
specific things that I will describe, he began to get specific
sexual pleasure from having them in his car. Then of course,
trapping them in the car by locking the handle, giving him
even greater control over their lives, or power over them. And
then particularly this power or control and domination of them
as he moved into remote rural areas; a bend in the road, and
so forth, a knife or a gun . . .

"In one instance," Fort said, "as one of the victims lay dying,
further sexual satisfaction occurred in his mind and he had
intercourse with her while she was still breathing. But in all of
the other instances as he described it to me, and as recon-
structed from the many records, they were already dead when
he engaged in feeling the breast and comparing their breasts
to his image of what an ideal female breast felt like and looked
like.

"His sexual pleasure went on to include stripping them and
voyeuristically just looking at this naked body. That element
of it included taking Polaroid photographs of them and of the
heads of several after he beheaded them.

"It included oral copulations with several of the victims, and
most of all it included what he described to me as violent, extremely exciting acts of penile vaginal intercourse where he
rapidly had orgasms and ejaculation.

"This was then followed in sort of a declining . . . sense of sexual pleasure by collecting their clothing, keeping some of it for varying periods of time, and collecting objects like books or other paraphernalia that they were carrying with them, and keeping them for varying periods of time, and glancing at them sometimes."

As Fort and the other experts continued, neither the defense nor the prosecution made a point of the medical significance of Kemper's necrophilia, although the acting out of it is an extremely rare phenomenon. Many persons are necrophilic to some degree (in a social sort of way), yet they do not engage in sex with the dead. In fact the worship of death is an extremely pervasive sickness in the American culture, manifested in many ways.

Fromm declares that the pure necrophile is insane.

Stekel, in his famed clinical studies on *Sadism and Masochism*, cites twenty-three cases of sexual gratification upon dead bodies cited by "Epaulard," Lyons, 1901. It did not astonish him to find that among this group were two medical students, one assistant in anatomy, two gravediggers, and a washer of bodies.

This study is interesting for the fact that in only two of the twenty-three cases did four acts occur: murder, intercourse, mutilation, and cannibalism. Kemper fitted in this rarest of groups—yet in the U.S.A. in 1973 a succession of eminent psychiatrists and psychologists were prepared to find him an ordinary garden variety of sociopath.

The necrophile is attracted to all that is dead or decaying, and comes alive when the conversation is about sickness, burials, and death. According to Fromm (*Heart of Man*), such persons live in the sentimental past rather than the future and tend to be cold, distant devotees of law-and-order. Their attitude toward force is characteristic: they see it in Simone Weil's definition as "the capacity to transform a man into a corpse."

Possessiveness in love is a common enough trait of Homo sapiens; but to the necrophile, it is everything, the only means he has of relating to the (dead) object or person that attracts him. If he loses the possessed, it is like a threat to himself and a severing of his contact with reality. This may help to explain why Kemper seemed driven in cyclical buildups of tension to the committing of fresh murders: his trophies of death eventually left him, were lost to him, through decay. He would feel his panic returning. The necrophile, as Fromm says, is "deeply afraid of life."

Stekel writes that the frequency with which *traces* of cannibalism and necrophilism occur, as expressed in the phobias and dreams of otherwise normal persons, would indicate that a time existed in mankind's development when "these impulses were permitted to appear openly," and he believes that they must be regarded as atavistic petrifactions.

Kemper, according to Dr. Fort, obtained particular excitement from postspecific acts: "Particular excitement from looking through their (the victims') identification, having various kinds of imagery about what their families might be like. On some occasions, including one I particularly remember, driving down to . . . Southern California, where one of the six victims had come from, and going past her family's house, and having thoughts about how he had struck back at them by killing their daughter, and even being tempted to phone them or make other contact with them."

Asked by the district attorney whether he believed the defendant had known "right from wrong at the time of his acts," Dr. Fort said he had, and that he had known "the nature and quality of his acts," and that he had been both "completely sane and . . . legally sane under California law." In all his killings, in Fort's opinion, he had been able to premeditate and deliberate, as well as "to meaningfully and maturely reflect upon the gravity of his acts."

Fort alluded to Kemper's physical problems. "This hatred and aggressiveness were intensified by his abnormality in the sense of excessive height that made him very self-conscious. I will say, to a lesser extent, being left-handed also contributed to his feelings of rejection."

Citing Kemper's painstaking efforts to remove evidence as part of his pattern, Fort said also, "He had displayed a special interest in and had studied police work, ballistics, and medicine, and particularly psychology and psychiatry, and how to fool the psychologists on tests . . . All of these things to me show very careful, very intelligently . . . and very intentionally conceived plans—not only to kill but to get away with the killings."

He discussed the range of mental disorders and their changing terminology. Asked in which diagnostic category he would place Kemper, he replied, "I would place him in the broader category of personality disorder, specifically antisocial personality, which is no more, and no less, than the old diagnosis of psychopath or sociopath. And particularly I would refer to him as a sexual sociopath, or as I said earlier, in common language, a sex maniac."

Asked to explain why the medical terminology had changed in recent years in these respects, he said with candor, "I think it reflects a movement in all professions for being more obscure and less intelligible to the general public. That's a way that some people have of showing how smart they are, by talking in a language that nobody else can understand."

But also, he said, U.S. psychiatrists believed that too much stigma was being attached to the word *psychopath* and that it did too much harm to individuals as a label. Preoccupation with civil rights also had helped to change it.

Dr. Fort defined the characteristics of a psychopath or sociopath in part as "not operating by any recognized or accepted moral code, but operating entirely according to expediency to what one feels like doing at the moment, or that which will give the individual the most gratification or pleasure. It includes an absence of conscience.

". . . All people are complicated and all people are a mixture of things, and what we are talking about is a relative absence of conscience . . . But generally the psychopath has little or no conscience . . . does not profit from experience in the usual sense, that is, does not modify his behavior to conform to societal standards."

He described this as the most common and pervasive of conditions with psychiatric labels and said that, because of this, society had a tendency, if someone did a bizarre thing, of translating it into craziness and then into schizophrenia.

Judge Brauer, fearful that the jury might find Kemper insane, questioned Fort's use of the word *maniac* as possibly misleading, saying it would ordinarily denote a very high degree of disturbance. Fort agreed, saying he had used the term only because it communicated the idea of crimes of major dimension that involved major psychopathy.

The psychopath or antisocial person, he said, was also often characterized by "gross selfishness and callousness," and by acts of cruelty at an early age. Kemper's record, he said, showed that the California Youth Authority doctors in 1964 had diagnosed him as a passive-aggressive person, which was consistent with his own diagnosis, and that one psychiatrist in that period had diagnosed him as paranoid schizophrenic—with which Fort disagreed.

The district attorney was pleased by this, since *he* wanted no intimation that Kemper had suffered from serious mental illness as a child.

Fort said, "It was one of the many mistakes that were made there."

(However, Dr. Vanasek, chief of research at Atascadero during Kemper's commitment there, said later that the very early history of fantasies about death and his cruelty to animals—contained in the record which Fort read—was very indicative of childhood schizophrenia.)

"The origin of the diagnosis, as far as I could trace it back," Fort said, "was two physicians, court examiners, in Madera County who in a—without any explanation whatsoever, just a brief one- or two-line statement—put down paranoid schizophrenia; and that record, that statement by them then led to the commitment, the subsequent institutionalization at Atascadero."

The two doctors, he said, "may or may not have had relevant background and experience."

To the spectator, it appeared that the single question Dr. Fort, the district attorney, and Judge Brauer unanimously wished to avoid was: "If schizophrenia made Edmund Kemper insane at the age of fourteen or fifteen, qualifying him for commitment (because *something* qualified him for commitment), and if he continued to have bizarre fantasies in the hospital and after his release, and shortly thereafter killed eight more persons in a bizarre and sadistic way—then how did he become so sane so suddenly?"

Not even the public defender seemed particularly interested in pushing this question.

"A paranoid schizophrenic," Fort continued, "should have marked feelings of unreality, depersonalization—meaning that you lose your sense of identity, and lose the boundaries between yourself and other people in your environment, and most of all, has delusions, meaning false beliefs, beliefs that you are being persecuted, beliefs that can be grandiose where you think you have enormous powers, and hallucinations, meaning seeing things or hearing things that aren't there."

Kemper, he insisted, showed none of these symptoms. He was not paranoid, because his grandmother and his mother *actually had been* rejecting of him and withholding of affection. (This was accepted even though the evidence of these women's attitudes had originated solely from interviews with Edmund. The dead had not spoken.) And Edmund had testified that he started killing young women when he got tired of people "walking on his head."

Although Fort found no evidence in Kemper of schizophrenic delusions of grandeur, he did a few minutes later describe Kemper's crimes as fitting in the category of magnicide, or an effort to commit the so-called "instant status" crime. This drive need not have been delusional, considering the pervasiveness of *Godfather*-worship in America; but *acting out* such crimes was not yet representative of the status quo. In fact, it was highly abnormal behavior.

The defendant, Dr. Fort said, "gets a considerable amount of pleasure and satisfaction from his status as a mass killer. . . . The recognition that he sometimes desperately sought as a child, the attempt to overcome rejection. Not being able to make it in any other way.

"I think he feels he has been compensated for it by the status he has gained. . . . If you do a big enough killing, either of a single individual like a president or a senator or a great enough number of lesser-known individuals, it instantly vaults you into prominence, and then what I will consider in a very perverse way, it makes you one more celebrity in a society that seems to be grabbing for celebrities . . .

"He described to me the way girls . . . and other people stare at him as he is brought to the courtroom and brought back to the jail. There are some instances where he has been asked for an autograph. He described to me, with a mixture of pleasure and some expression of regret, the write-ups that have occurred. And he spoke of the attention he got as a special prisoner in the jail, how 'everything is special handling' for him.

"And my conclusion from that, and from the tape, was that one of the important motivations was the recognition, the glory, the sensational attention that he gets as a mass murderer."

Asked if he had any opinions as to why Kemper had killed his grandparents as a teenager, Fort said, "Again, I don't think it was for any one reason, but the major things were that he saw them—particularly his grandmother—as an extremely harsh authoritative-type lady who did not care for him, did not let him do any of the things that he wanted to do, was keeping him against his will because he preferred to be with his father, and if not with his father, with his mother.

"And another factor for that killing was that she was a symbol of two people that he hated and rejected for different reasons. Particularly she was very much like his mother in her personality and reactions to him, came on in the same way to him subjectively as his mother did; and she, of course, being the mother of his father, was very closely tied together with his father, whom he resented for having abandoned him at an early age and having rejected him whenever he sought contact with the father.

". . . I think the killing of the grandfather was, again, for several reasons. Somewhat different. He saw him also as not letting him do the things that he or other boys his age should have been allowed to do. He certainly didn't seem as harsh and as punitive as the grandmother, but he shared some of the dimension of keeping him there against his will and making him do things that he didn't like. But also it was an effort to cover up . . . was self-protection . . ."

Fort said he had discussed with Kemper the killing of the cats and dogs at an early age—because they would not obey him—which he found consistent with the diagnosis of a sociopath-psychopath.

Kemper had told Fort about fantasies of killing his sisters and other people at an early age. "It was mainly his older sister, but sometimes it involved the younger one. She had friends, got more attention, respect, and affection from the mother. In general, she had the things he didn't have.

"But I must add that that did not seem to be a predominant part of his thinking during that time, certainly as compared to his hatred of his mother, thoughts of killing her or thoughts he would often have about killing the boys who teased him or would not play with him, and so forth."

Dr. Fort commented on Kemper's ability to talk about "extremely destructive and horrible kinds of behavior . . . in a very natural and open manner without showing any emotion, any reaction to it, without any compassion or guilt being expressed about it."

Under the district attorney's questioning, he added that although Kemper had made suicide attempts in jail, he was not in his opinion truly suicidal, which "isn't to say that it wouldn't be possible for him, ar anybody else, to commit suicide." And he held to this position even when Kemper appeared in court with his face reddened by Mace burns received when the guards had attempted to intervene in the ballpoint-pen attempt.

When Fort had talked to Kemper earlier, he said, the defendant had "specifically showed no signs of depression or any suicidal thoughts. And . . . he specifically told me in a number of different ways and times that he would never kill himself, that he wanted to get the gas chamber, and that if necessary he will kill somebody else (in prison) . . . so that he can legally get the gas chamber. And as part of that thought, some of which he has had since childhood about getting the gas chamber, he voted for the death penalty last November."

This seemed the most curious part of Dr. Fort's testimony—his discounting the childhood effort of the defendant to jump off the Empire State Building, his depressions since the murder of his mother, the attempts on his own life in prison, his voting for the death penalty, his wish for legal extermination. While the last two are not directly suicidal, the end to be achieved is surely the same. And it was necrophilia all the way, both for the "hunted and the hunter," to use Kemper's favorite terminology.

Public Defender James Jackson questioned him on these points. Kemper, he said, had actually slashed his wrist and lost two pints of blood.

Fort replied that he was merely trying to get more attention.

Again, as to Fort's statement that the defendant had shown no remorse, the defender asked if Kemper had not cried three times while under the truth serum. Fort replied that that would not necessarily indicate remorse.

"But he did cry?" asked Jackson.

"Very briefly and insignificantly," replied the court's dispassionate witness.

Jackson persisted, "Do you recall that after he got back in the San Mateo Jail after the sodium amytal test, he banged his head on the wall of the jail and cried for two days off and on?"

"I recall," Dr. Fort replied, "that he needed special treatment and was reporting discouragement and depression. I saw that more as an effect of the amytal and the methadrine that the doctors also gave him, which is a potent amphetamine . . . and not in any way related to any feelings or remorse . . ."

"Why," asked Jackson, "does he want to go and sit in a gas chamber?"

"The single biggest reason," Fort said, "again I think there would be many factors entering into it—but the single biggest one is that it relates to his concept of magnicide that I mentioned earlier. He recalled to me that in childhood, and I think it was about the age of eight, he paid particular attention to the execution of a woman who had hired some killers, I think it

was, in California, and he began to have—that's his first recol-
lection of the gas chamber, and it became tied together in his
mind with his general and specific violence and aggressiveness.

"And more recently, I believe it to be tied together with the
status that he sees himself as having ... particularly as a sexual
killer of young, attractive women."

It was perhaps unfortunate that Jackson, irritated as he was
by Fort, shared his chic contempt for the medical terminology.
Stekel and Fromm would have found the clues to Kemper's
death-love occurring far earlier than his eighth year, and not
in later dreams of magnicide.

Judge Brauer, alert to any suggestion to the jury that Kemper
might have wanted to go sit in the gas chamber because he
suffered from a touch of madness, said, "Mr. Jackson, whether
he is *mentally ill* is not the issue in this case."

Jackson said, "It is partly. It is one of the elements of insanity."

"Well, it is not the same as insanity," the judge replied. "I
just want to make sure that the jury doesn't get the wrong
impression ..."

Under the truth serum Kemper had produced fresh details
of horror which Dr. Fort now described.

"One piece of information about cannibalism that he commits
with the bodies of the coeds came out in the amytal interview,
that I have not found anywhere else, and which he had not
personally discussed with me ... As part of dismembering and
cutting the bodies of the girls after he killed them. He took,
with some of them—it was unclear how many pieces of their
flesh—cooked it and ate it."

At the end of the direct examination, Judge Brauer, still
worried that the jury might be having trouble with definitions,
asked Dr. Fort whether the various psychiatric categories he
had discussed all denoted the same degree of mental disturbance.

"Some ... denote hardly any degree of mental disturbance?"
Judge Brauer asked.

"Psychiatric diagnoses," Dr. Fort reassured him, "in general
are so all-encompassing. Various studies have been done; one

familiar one called the Midtown Manhattan Study—they found ninety percent of the population to be mentally or emotionally ill. You are quite right. Some of the categories are so broad as to be in my concept 'meaningless'; but there is another thing— the diagnoses are not in any way tied with social problems.

"That is, they exist in a vacuum, and the diagnosis in no way would reflect whether the person had killed, burglarized, wire-tapped, or committed any other antisocial acts."

Dr. Fort was critical of the "easy availability of handguns in our society, both from gun shops and from friends," as increasing the likelihood that a man with Kemper's interest in weapons would become a more efficient killer.

He added that in his opinion, if Kemper were allowed to go free, he "would kill again, and kill the same kind of victim."

Jackson queried him about a statement Kemper had made to the California Youth Authority as a teenager in which, "He described evil forces within him which tried to control his behavior.

"What," he asked, "do you make of that?"

But Fort was not to be sidetracked into the mists of demonology. The teenager, he said, had been trying to find an explanation for what he had done, was confused about it, and lacked enough understanding of himself.

The psychiatrist further refused to go along with Jackson's suggestion that the boy's mention of evil forces might be significant of delusion.

Fort said confidently also that, although Kemper had deceived other doctors, he could not have fooled him. Fort had been alert to trickery.

Asked why he had not learned directly from Kemper about his cannibalism, Fort said he had not attempted to explore the extreme boundaries of deviant behavior, since "to pursue that would have been a relatively small detail."

Jackson asked if the defendant had disclosed to Fort that he had put his mother's head on a mantelpiece and yelled at it.

"No."

"Did he tell you that he threw darts at his mother's head?"

"No."

"Did he tell you that he put her larynx down the garbage disposal?"

"Yes," Fort said. "He also told me about cutting it out, and in that way getting back at her for all of the bitter things she had said to him over the years." The things he had not been told, he said, were "basically irrelevant to the more important things we talked about . . ."

Jackson cited other aspects of Kemper's assault after death upon his mother's body, seeking to show that Dr. Fort too had been manipulated by the defendant, but Fort stood by his position that this was highly unlikely.

And to get back at Jackson, Fort volunteered the information that Kemper had told him that he had planned to plead guilty, but that it had been the public defender's advice to him that he plead Not Guilty by Reason of Insanity.

Throughout the trial, *no* doctor alluded to the medical significance of Kemper's childhood death fantasies, suicide attempts, cat-killings, and doll-mutilations as possible evidence of a mental disease that might have impaired his ability to know right from wrong in the eight murders committed after his release from Atascadero.

One of the early questions about Kemper's crimes, with his powerful feelings of hatred for his mother, was why he had not killed her first of all. The conjecture of journalists and others was that, had he done so, his murderous drive might have fizzled out.

Dr. Don Lowe explained it this way:

"As the months went by and as efforts to be successful in ordinary ways of relating to women were not successful, and whereas he had a large interest in women, and was turned on by them a good deal . . . the fantasy about his mother began to generalize to younger and attractive girls; he began to rationalize: 'Why think of killing my mother if there are young and attractive girls around?' "

Kemper had told Lowe that he fantasized about killing literally thousands of girls before commiting his first crime of this type. He had mentioned a childhood fantasy in which he had been able to turn people into dolls—which would not hurt him and which he could manipulate—"and in a sense that's kind of, in my mind, kind of an omnipotent quality."

This in fact was one of the very qualities Fort had said might signify schizophrenia, which he felt Kemper had never suffered from.

Dr. Lowe commented on Kemper's "sense of workmanship" that came through as he talked.

"He really did get quite animated about how quickly he could do a person in, or there certainly was a quality of workmanship, almost . . . Towards the end, he began to fantasize or think of doing things like leaving heads across from the police station."

Kemper had also entertained the wry notion of getting even with his mother, prior to the fateful Easter weekend, by picking up the telephone in her presence, calling the police, and saying, "Hello, I'm the coed killer."

Jackson suggested to the expert witness that Kemper's outstanding work record at Atascadero might have had a manipulative goal.

"If you have been trying, with an I.Q. of a superior range, to get out of a mental hospital by showing that you are sane, you are covering up your insanity, aren't you?"

Dr. Lowe's reply hit one of the basic flaws in the sanity/insanity rules.

"Well," he said, "in a sense that's almost the definition of sanity, according to many people, the ability to—you know, to *act* sane. So it is a difficult question. People could say that most of us go around with a bag of worms, but we are able to act reasonably well and do the things we do, and we get by."

Judge Brauer again intervened for the sake of clarity, saying, "Aren't we making an assumption there, Mr. Jackson, that he was in fact insane?"

"Well, it is legally presumed that he *was* insane, having been committed there," Jackson replied.

Lowe might have added to his "almost" definition of sanity the changing concepts of abnormal behavior in a nation where potential violence increasingly was becoming an accepted fact of every citizen's life. If Kemper were found sane, could it not be assumed that the acceptable "norm" in 1974 was reversion to the period in mankind's development when cannibalism, necrophilism, murder, and mutilation were socially all right? For Lowe was saying that common usage or custom established the norm, and Jackson too appeared to subscribe to that view.

But when Jackson said, "Isn't mental illness nothing more than society's definition of what society does not want or will not tolerate—for whatever reason?" Dr. Lowe, appearing to contradict himself, said, "No, I won't buy that."

Dr. Lowe, from his interviews with Kemper, did not believe he had "fooled" the doctors at Atascadero into granting an early release.

"It's my impression that at that time he really did feel that he had a chance to do well and to get out and live a good life; that he felt that he could in fact lead a decent and productive life when he left Atascadero, and that the staff . . . perceived that in him."

Dr. Lowe diagnosed Kemper as suffering from "character disorder-sexual deviation."

This is one of the accepted diagnoses in the *Diagnostic and Statistical Manual of Mental Disorders* published by the American Psychiatric Society.

Jackson said, "Do you remember the definition of sexual deviation being as follows: 'Even though many find their practices distasteful, they remain unable to substitute normal sexual behavior for them.'? Why are they unable to substitute normal sexual behavior?"

"It does seem that sexual drive and the objects of the drive are formed fairly early in life," Lowe said, "or begin formation fairly early in life, and . . . they become established and become very difficult to modify later on, but not entirely without success."

Jackson: "So when Mr. Kemper in the beginning of his sexual awareness, when he fantasizes beheading a grammar school teacher in order to kiss her—that is something that is very difficult for him to discard later in life. Correct?"

Dr. Lowe said he thought it would be.

And later in life, Jackson went on, he would not be thinking maturely but would still be thinking like an eight-year-old?

"Well," Lowe replied, "the drive itself, in my opinion, wouldn't necessarily reflect on the ability to control it."

Dr. Lowe, on redirect examination, said that he too thought the diagnosis of Kemper at age fifteen as schizophrenic had been incorrect and that the majority of people who had evaluated him at Atascadero had not seen him as a schizophrenic.

Lowe said he had tried his best to learn whether Kemper's fantasies were of such a nature and extent that he was really out of contact with reality.

"I didn't feel at any point," he said, "that his fantasies took over, that he lost the ability to differentiate those from ordinary external events. That he was always aware that they were fantasies, that they were his own personal, private things, that they were different than the world at large."

He believed that Kemper realized the enormity of his fantasies and acts. He found no evidence, moreover, of organic brain disease in the defendant.

It was as if everyone were afraid to find out that something was really wrong with the defendant; and this was the fault of the requirements of the judicial system. Nor was Judge Brauer to be blamed that an obsolete concept of law required him to remind the jury over and over again that they were governed in their decision by an idiotic rule originally created to define the very nature of "legal" idiocy.

No more risks could be run with a two-time loser like Kemper—as he himself had well known when he started killing again. Even had it been found that he suffered from brain damage or defect, it is most unlikely he would have been sent to a mental hospital rather than to a prison—although it might have spared him the death penalty had that been in effect.

What society wanted to know about Kemper had nothing to do with whether he fitted in one or other of those noncategories, *sane* or *insane*, but rather 1) whether he had committed the crimes as charged, and 2) whether he deserved more to be punished or pitied. In any case the public must be protected from him for the remainder of his life—which ruled out sending him back to a mental hospital.

When obscure and misleading distinctions are allowed to remain in the law, they do positive harm by diverting public attention from the reality of the dilemma—and this is true in the case of M'Naghten.

It is almost a natural law that whenever falsehood is locked into the rules of the system, social harm results. Here one sector of our social organization—the law—makes it impossible for another sector—medicine—to look deeply into illness and thus help the public understand its nature and causes. Without public understanding the illness will continue.

A sweeping, highly controversial revision of the Federal Criminal Code was proposed by congress in the 1980's that would change, among other things, the whole nature of the insanity defense. Defendants who are successful in the future in proving insanity could still be found guilty and sent to prison under the proposed revision, rather than found not guilty and committed to a mental hospital.

In a sense, this particular section of the proposed code is merely recognition of the current widespread practice of finding a mentally ill killer sane for the specific purpose of confining him in a maximum security prison. It recognizes an existing reality, rather than ducking it.

Yet the idea of a modern, civilized nation imprisoning a very sick person is repugnant. It was repugnant in Victorian times. Like the death penalty itself, the effect on the population at large cannot help but be brutalizing, unless—and this is a very big if—it forces complete reform of our prisons. Protecting the public and providing medical help to a sick person need not be mutually exclusive. But punishment *would* be exclusive. Governor Edmund G. Brown, Jr. of California noted that U.S. prisons are mainly for punishment and that we delude ourselves if we think of them as rehabilitative. It goes without saying that we delude ourselves if we think of them as providing adequate medical care for very sick inmates.

One way of remedying the problem might be to limit the responsibility of the lay jury simply to determining whether or not a defendant is guilty, not of a degree of murder but of the fact of killing. If guilty, the facts of the crime and medical records could be presented to an experienced professional panel composed of medical and correctional authorities empowered to dispose of the case, the defendant to be represented by counsel in both phases of the proceeding. The panel would be guided 1) by society's right to protection; 2) by society's right to inflict appropriate punishment; and 3) by the medical/behavioral prognosis of the defendant. Whatever disposition is made, psychiatric care ought to be available to prisoners who wish it.

For most offenders, the loss of freedom is itself the cruelest punishment, but apparently this is not universally true.

Chief Assistant Public Defender Jackson, who had worked for several years as a deputy district attorney in the high-crime area of Alameda county and who had helped convict as well as defend hardened criminals, told me he believed that many offenders repeat their crimes because they are able to obtain virtually everything they want in prison, including sex (but usually not female); are bored on the outside; like to be told every move they are supposed to make; and are so desensitized that their loss of freedom means little to them. Such hardened criminals, he says, as a rule do not want what is offered them in the way of educational opportunities and rehabilitation. Often as soon as they get out, they do something to get back in. And Jackson thinks the answer—taking human differences into account—is to make them work, make prison less pleasant for them. He is quick to acknowledge that few humanitarians would agree.

Jessica Mitford (*Kind and Unusual Punishment*) would likely retort that the opportunities for rehabilitation and medical care in a large prison are virtually nil; that the indeterminate sentence makes hardened criminals of the young and malleable by destroying hope; and that most prisoners would never have been committed in the first place had they been judged by the same standards as are the perpetrators of white, middle-class crime.

Dr. Karl Menninger and many others who have studied crime and punishment believe that simply condemning an offender to spend the rest of his life in a cell the size of a small bathroom is itself cruel and unusual punishment and that most maximum-security prisons in the U.S. are atrocious.

In the topsy-turvy world of Edmund Kemper, however, where the better part of life was death and all of its mementos, where the free world was a terrifying place, it can be argued that society rewarded rather than punished him by offering him thick prison walls and the potential—if he ever managed to kill a guard—of execution.

The trial of Edmund Kemper lasted three weeks, but it took the jury only five hours to reach a decision.

Defender Jackson, in a final effort to do his professional best by a client he had never asked for, told jurors in his closing argument, "There are two people locked up in the body of this young giant, one good and one evil . . . One is fighting to be here with us and the other is slipping off to his own little world of fantasy where he is happy."

When the jury returned, Kemper showed no emotion as Judge Brauer read the verdict: "Guilty, Sane, and First Degree' to all eight counts."

The judge sentenced Kemper to life in prison and told him that he was going to recommend "in the strongest terms possible" that he not be released for "the rest of your natural life."

During the period when Kemper had been transported to and from the San Mateo County Jail for trial, he had become acquainted with a slightly built Santa Cruz County sheriff's deputy named Bruce Colomny, a man not much older than himself. Colomny had been kind to the gigantic defendant. Although no one would ever have confused the deputy with John Wayne, he nevertheless represented another father figure to Kemper.

"He's more like a father to me than anyone I have ever known," he said. "He's like the father I wish I had had."

Slowly he removed the precious Junior Chamber of Commerce pin from the lapel of his buckskin jacket.

Colomny described this episode, a scene that would have wrenched the heart of any B-grade movie fan.

"Ed looked at it for a long time and tears came to his eyes. Then he handed it to me and said, 'Here, I want you to have it.' "

Although Kemper had professed a desire for the death penalty (which he probably did not get only because of the hiatus in its application, it being reinstated two months after his conviction), it galled him that Herbie Mullin drew first degree murder on only two counts.

"You know," he said, "it really sticks in my craw that Mullin only got two 'firsts' and I got eight. He was just a cold-blooded killer, running over a three-week period, killing everybody he saw for no good reason." (This despite his statement in court that he thought Mullin insane.)

Then he laughed.

"I guess that's kind of hilarious, my sitting here so self-righteously talking like that, after what I've done."

Before Kemper went off to prison—where he said he planned to spend his time in tight security studying and reading—he expressed the hope that he might find a way to help other people. "Maybe they can study me," he said, "and find out what makes people like me do the things they do."

Whether he meant this sincerely at the time, it is hard to say; but later as I discovered in communicating to him the interest of doctors in doing just that, his attitude had changed.

He continued to try to psyche out his interviewers until the very end.

"You haven't asked the questions I expected a reporter to ask," he told writer Marj von Beroldingen (*Front Page Detective*, March 1974). "What is it like to have sex with a dead body? . . . What does it feel like to sit on your living room couch and look over and see two decapitated girls' heads on the arms of the couch?" He paused and then supplied a partial answer, "The first time, it makes you sick to your stomach."

Then he proposed another question and gave his answer, obviously relishing the discomfort his candor was causing: "What do you think, now, when you see a pretty girl walking down the street? One side of me says, 'Wow, what an attractive chick. I'd like to talk to her, date her.' The other side of me says, 'I wonder how her head would look on a stick?'"

To von Beroldingen's dismay, he switched suddenly from his animated manner to an expression of withdrawal and the reliving of acts of violence. Previously he had told her that he considered his actions those of a demented person. Now (alone with her in his cell), he began to illustrate just how he had killed Mrs. Hallett, a mature woman like his interviewer. He straightened up in his chair.

"I came up behind her and crooked my arm around her neck, like this," he said, bending his powerful arm in front of himself at chin level. "I squeezed and just lifted her off the floor. She just hung there, and for a moment, I didn't realize she was dead . . . I had broken her neck and her head was just wobbling around, with the bones of her neck disconnected in the skin sack of her neck."

To the interviewer's horror, Kemper began to wobble his head around, never changing the position of his arms, and gazing fixedly at her. His pale face had become slightly flushed, his breath came quickly, and he began to stutter.

She broke the evil spell by fumbling for cigarettes and by uttering some disarming (as it were) comment. In a moment they were again talking on a light note and she accepted Kemper's courteous invitation to dine with him in the cell. They parted on a bantering note.

James Jackson said candidly after the trial that Kemper was probably "medically insane," the jury's ruling resulting from fear. In any event, neither he nor any of the several psychologists and psychiatrists who had examined Kemper or treated him in the past quarreled with the verdict.

He was sent to the Vacaville Medical Facility for observation and processing and then to the maximum security prison at Folsom.

CHAPTER SEVENTEEN

DIAGNOSTIC ERROR?

WHEN THE CELL DOOR slammed on Edmund Emil Kemper, III for the second time in his young life, society was more than eager to forget him. The many whose lives had been devastated by his acts could only hope that time might bring some easing of pain, some blurring of memory. For society as a whole, apparently nothing was to be learned from his brief and bitter passage. The judicial system had disposed of one more sociopathic personality or disordered personality—whatever *they* were—and seemed content. Another killer put away. Good riddance.

It was plain that Kemper had messed up partly because a few people had erred flagrantly—as he had always been the first to admit. Like many persons who never formally qualify as criminals, he could always place the responsibility for his acts elsewhere. For what he had done after his release from Atascadero, he blamed in part society, the courts, the doctors, the agencies, and of course his parents. He also blamed his parole officer.

"I didn't have the supervision I should have had once I got out," he complained. "I was supposed to see my parole officer every other week and a social worker the other week. I never did. I think if I had, I would have made it. Two weeks after I was on the streets, I got scared because I hadn't seen anyone. Finally, I called the district parole office and asked if I was doing something wrong . . . Was I supposed to go to my parole officer, or would he come to see me, I asked." Kemper said the man on the phone had asked, "What's the matter, you got a problem?" And Kemper had replied that he had not.

Then, according to him, the person said, "Well, we're awfully busy with people who have. We'll get to you."

In fact the person in charge of Kemper's case in Santa Cruz County was regarded by those who knew him around the court-house as a most conscientious person who undoubtedly would have helped had he been aware of Kemper's build-up of tensions, just as Dr. Schanberger in San Luis Obispo would have done.

But to expect an assumption of initiative where it does not exist is a socially bootless business. As Dr. Marvin Ziporyn, who treated mass murderer Richard Speck, noted, the law assumes that every citizen is responsible for his conduct, that if he so chooses he can be good, and if he is bad "it is pure cussedness." It is unlikely, however, that anyone would choose to be a social outcast and a criminal, *given* the choice, or that he would elect to be born to cruel or indifferent or poverty-stricken parents, or to be afflicted at birth with damage to his central nervous system, or any of a multitude of possible misfortunes that often afflict an emerging criminal.

Ziporyn, who admits that he is a "determinist," says that at first when reading in the papers of some chilling murder, he would think of the killer as evil incarnate; but usually later on he would find, as in the case of Speck, "a dependent, love-seeking, emotionally disturbed, miserably unhappy member of the human family."*

Some of the officers who knew Kemper had a similar reaction to him and found it almost impossible to believe that he had committed the crimes to which he confessed.

But others pegged him as "conwise," and as a "cold, sadistic killer," who presumably, could have changed his ways had he tried.

In any event, vengeance and punishment were unlikely to advance society's understanding of violence, and they were unlikely to help parents spot the danger signs of a potentially violent person in the early years of childhood.

Dr. David Abrahamsen considers violence a characteristic form of American expression that is especially exacerbated during times of economic and social upheaval.

He and other observers of deviant behavior have isolated some of the signs that should send parents or school teachers in search of medical help for the child. Inherent in the difficulty, however, is the possibility that both parents will to a greater or lesser degree be part of the problems to which they should be alert.

Among the signs: cruelty to animals, excessive aggressiveness and temper tantrums, feelings of parental deprivation or mother domination, lying, arson, petty stealing, violent acts, loneliness, withdrawal, exposure to violent behavior in family, exposure to parental incest, recurrent fantasies of revenge and omnipotence, excessive truancy, low threshold to frustration, self-destructiveness, accident proneness, psychosomatic symptoms, speech and spelling errors, bedwetting, and abnormal sex chromosomes. Such children often have received severe head injuries.

Not all problems will be present in an individual; but the presence of two or more should alert the parent. In many

---

* Jack Altman and Marvin Ziporyn, M.D., *Born to Raise Hell* (New York: Grove Press, Inc., 1967).

cases, a violent person is reared in a family where the mother is strong and aggressive and the father, when not absent from home altogether, is weak and irresponsible.

But sometimes the home situation may be even more dangerous—an absent or alcoholic father and an equally weak mother so depressed and overwhelmed by the needs of several children that she is unable to give proper attention to any of them. Then the most needful of the brood is likely to find himself being shuffled at an early age through the bewildering network of institutions and agencies designed to test, process, and house the delinquent juvenile. It may be that *no* amount of such professional help will compensate a disturbed child for the elemental need for a secure home—even when the "danger signs" are detected in time. It is possible—indeed, likely— that our approach to the early heading off of criminal violence may be caught up in at least one of the same basic errors that characterized U.S. involvement in the Vietnam War: the pouring of good money after ineffective money.

Consider the case of a fourteen-year-old "recidivist" named John* in New York—who has committed the crimes of criminal possession of a dangerous weapon and attempted sodomy of an eight-year-old boy—with a family background of the type described above, who in 1975, cost the taxpayers $20,00 per year for residential institutions, through which he was funneled, *in addition* to the huge costs of processing him through endless agencies. And John was still considered a "lost" child, like thousands of others in the city. The best prognoses are that such children grow up to rape, mug, and murder at an even more astronomical social and financial cost.

Question: If the money were handed over to John's depressed family in full each year as a "grant for a secure home" (much as smaller sums are handed over for educational scholarships), rather than being filtered away through the papier maché bureaucracy of social welfare, what would be the effect?

* Reported in *The New York Times*, May 7, 1975. Today the costs are much higher.

Surely the stability to be purchased might imbue the family with a sense of pride and relative safety that could never be purchased with a welfare check. It might provide for summer vacations, a family car, the beginnings of a savings account. As it is, the taxpayers' hard-earned money is largely wasted, and crime continues, and children go on being "lost."

But the apparent rewarding of fecklessness and bad luck go deeply against the American grain. Even murder is less repugnant, especially since it usually happens to someone else.

Perhaps it is true—as the psychologists and psychiatrists said when trying to explain how Edmund Kemper could so easily have been released from a mental hospital to resume his murderous career—that the ultimate solutions to crime lie with the public's education. But maybe the citizen already knows in his heart where the answers lie and what they are and subconsciously prefers high crime rates and wasted taxes to the alternatives, which would leave him with fewer scapegoats and fewer legitimate gripes. Also, it makes a lot of citizens feel good, feel vindicated, when a Kemper gets sent up for life or gets the chair.

Certainly in putting Edmund Kemper out of sight and mind, society had not seemed particularly interested in understanding why a highly intelligent, six-foot-nine-inch youth had become a mass murderer instead of an athlete; why a young man who seemed so fixed on all the square, middle-class verities had not in fact honored his Junior Chamber of Commerce pin by trying to build up a small business, say a motorcycle repair or supply shop; why he had not married the immature, passive high school girl and educated himself in man/woman sex in the safety of her unalarming arms; and raised children, and bought trailbikes to carry around on his camper; and lived happily ever after.

Why *had* he blown it? If he had been able to get through a transitional few years of adjustment, building confidence in an ability to cope with the outside world, might his life thereafter have been different? Might ten persons now be alive?

One who shared the writer's feeling of unanswered

questions that could be important, and of frustration that many lives had been wasted yet nothing learned, was Dr. Vanasek. I called on him in his new position as director of admission at the "recycled" Patton State Hospital, down where the smog and the orange groves meet in San Bernardino County.

Vanasek's research field is sexual deviation. He is often called upon to testify as a forensic expert in criminal cases.

I found him a warm, enthusiastic man whose fascination with his work had conveyed itself to an unusually dedicated staff; and I was taken first of all on a tour of R and T (receiving and treatment) by Irma Smith, RN, who heads the training program.

Then we talked about the Kemper case—the feeling of "unfinishedness" about the trial.

Although Dr. Vanasek had gotten to know the teenaged Kemper very well, he said, "The person you really ought to talk with is Dr. Schanberger at San Luis Obispo, who saw him every day in the lab where Kemper worked as crew leader."

In Atascadero, he said, "Kemper was treated as a psychopath or sociopath, but in my opinion the pride he took in his work was not typical of that."

He affirmed that, with what they knew of Kemper at the time, however, he had received the best medical care available.

They had not had the information that later emerged in trial testimony—the details of extreme mutilation of bodies, necrophilia, cannibalism, and even the extent of his childhood fantasies and cruelty to animals as revealed by his sister.

Vanasek could only hypothesize, but to him it seemed that this put a drastically new light on matters.

He spoke of Kemper's resentment of orders from women and speculated that the victims had tried to tell him to do something.

"That was certainly true," I said, "in the first case of Mary Ann," and told him of Kemper's rage when she began trying to use methods of reasoning that reminded him of his Atascadero experience. "But he meant to kill her anyhow."

As we talked over the evidence presented at the trial, Dr. Vanasek said, "I would be willing to make an educated guess that he was not a sociopath but a classic sadist, which is a sexual deviation; that he may have been exposed to some parental sexual experience of a traumatic nature as a child, which is one of the most disturbing things that can happen to a person. In addition there would likely have been exposure as a child to a 'punishing' type of religion—one of the physically flagellating kind. His early childhood experiences are all-important in understanding what happened."

Kemper's severing of his mother's head, he said, might well have been related to such a traumatic childhood experience. And his sexual assault on his mother's body after death was not, in his opinion, as some had speculated, an effort to "return to the womb." Had it been that, he said, Kemper would have cut her open and literally returned.

"He claimed to have been converted to Christianity in his adolescence," I said. "He read the Bible, and the character he most identified with was Job."

Vanasek nodded.

"If your hypothesis is correct, would it have changed things insofar as his treatment at Atascadero was concerned?" I asked.

"If we had had the knowledge that has come out since the recent murders," he said, "the Atascadero diagnosis might well have been classic sadism. Then he would not have been considered a good risk for release. There is no effective treatment for sadism because hospitals are not permitted to use aversion therapy strong enough to counter the sadistic drives, which are extremely powerful and deeply rooted."

I mentioned Kemper's having looked up his father after getting out of the hospital, and on the way home having picked up two girls and pictured how they would look without their heads. Six months later he had committed his first new murder. Vanasek said there might have been latent homosexuality, since he frequented the off-duty policemen's bar, yearned for his rejecting father, and professed a strong dislike of long-haired hippies. The early death fantasies and cruelty were typical, he said, of childhood schizophrenia.

Dr. Vanasek also commented that the medical investigations of the California Youth Authority, as passed on to mental hospitals, were usually extremely careful and reliable.

Although Kemper had spoken of murderous rages toward various boys and men, Vanasek said the significant point was that he had never attacked another male. His natural victims were young females, and the focus of his rage was the domineering mother.

"Where crimes are tied in with alcohol or drugs," he said, "the risk of repeating is almost certain if the patient or prisoner returns to a similar environment. In Kemper's case this did not apply. But he did return to the environment thought to cause his problems—being around his mother again and her being quite a domineering woman, apparently."

He stressed, however, the extreme efforts of readjustment needed of a patient accustomed to a controlled and dependent environment, in leaving a hospital after a long period. On the outside Kemper had had to find work, go to school, support himself, get reacquainted with a world that seemed almost foreign—and he had no work experience whatever, except inside the hospital. So he had returned to his mother.

"The criterion of a successful treatment program," Vanasek said, "is follow-up in the community after the patient's release. One of the biggest problems we have is that unless it is done on a voluntary basis by an individual hospital, as we do here at Patton, there is no provision in California for statistical review and analysis of mental patients, or a follow-up of them after release."

I left with his urging me again to get in touch with Dr. Schanberger. "Kemper should be studied," he said. "He could be very important to us."

Schanberger, when I communicated with him and asked how he felt about the case, said he was satisfied with the outcome of the trial since he could think of nothing better—but that from a medical standpoint, as one of those responsible for Kemper's treatment during a crucial period of his life, he remained frustrated and dissatisfied.

James Jackson had telephoned him from the public defender's office before the trial, asking him to testify for Kemper; but Schanberger said he had been unable to support a plea based on the legal definition of insanity.

I told him of Dr. Vanasek's hypothesis, based on the new evidence that had emerged at the trial. He expressed interest in discussing it against the background of Kemper's medical history at Atascadero, provided I obtained a release from Kemper to do so.

When I wrote to Kemper at Vacaville and asked for such a release, however, it appeared that he was no longer interested in trying to balance his accounts by helping society understand "what makes people like me do the things they do."

The written reply came from the program administrator of the California Medical Facility at Vacaville and conveyed a vehement refusal by the prisoner to grant such a release to Dr. Schanberger, which of course ended the possibility of a medical dialogue.

The unit psychiatrist at Vacaville reported with bureaucratic finality that the prisoner was "adjusting satisfactorily to institutionalization."

James Jackson told me that he could remember no evidence emerging from his and Harold Cartwright's many hours of interviews with Kemper to support the theory propounded as a possibility by Dr. Vanasek, except of course the well-known facts of the case. Perhaps characteristically, he also hazarded the opinion that the Atascadero psychologists were just looking for a way "to get off the hook."

I felt bound to refute this, pointing out that they had seemed willing enough to admit that an error might have occurred, provided the evidence warranted it.

"Anyhow," Jackson said, "I wasn't aware that there was a separate diagnosis called 'classic sadism.' These terms are all meaningless, in my opinion."

Was it really of no importance to learn the nature and causes

of Kemper's abnormality and to understand whether or not his
acts had been motivated by drives so compelling that he might
have been literally unable to resist them?

There was a growing tendency among young, liberal
behavioral scientists like Dr. Marlowe at UCSC to subscribe
to the Szaszian view of mental illness. Dr. Thomas S. Szasz
considered mental sickness a myth, an effort to assign to some
specific ill the blame for antisocial behavior, or as in the case
of witch-burning, the age-old search for scapegoats. And R.D.
Laing tells us that the whole scene is topsy-turvy. With society
crazy as it is, we still educate our children to conform to the
"normal." Therefore it follows that the patient who winds up
in a mental hospital with a breakdown is 1) perspicacious to
have flipped out and 2) healthier than ever if he can flip back
in with an even stronger, colder, and more uncompromising
view of reality.

Similarly Dr. William Glasser, who developed the thera-
peutic approach called Reality Therapy, discounts the concept
of mental illness. But he sees it as a mere prop enabling the
patient to continue passing the buck. He advocates dealing
directly with the patient's social problems. To Glasser, "all
that needs to be diagnosed is whether the patient is suffering
from irresponsibility or from an organic illness." He advocates
substituting the word irresponsibility for schizophrenia, and
his many followers have found doing so effective.

Yet there is a medical condition suffered by patients who
are sometimes called schizophrenic, and the use of mega-
vitamins, including the B vitamins with niacin, has been found
to cause marked improvement. It is also quite widely believed
that schizophrenic tendencies can be inherited.

This smorgasbord of conflicting medical opinion is offered
not by way of adding to the confusion but merely to empha-
size that, with the art in its present state, it is probably ludi-
crous for the courts to continue trying to establish sanity vs.
insanity. And to underscore the need for deeper insights—not
just to the mind as a fragile system within a vacuum but as
inseparable from the problems of the physical body; and to the
latter in turn within the social body. Stress is good for

us—up to a point. So is competition, until it turns us into cowards and bullies. At what point, for each person, do they become destructive—as they certainly do? President Harry Truman after a moment's reflection once told an anxious small boy who had asked if he had been "popular" in school, "Actually, I was kind of a sissy when I was your age." How can we make it easy, as it should be, for *anyone* to say, with the weight of science and social approval behind him, and without first having to grow up, and to be elected President of the United States, and to put a sign on his desk that says, "The buck stops here"—to say quite simply, "Don't press me, man," or "Help!" or, "That body contact stuff doesn't send me," or "What's so heroic about killing somebody if you've got the biggest gun?" or, perhaps, "It's *smart* to be a sissy. You could grow up to be President."

Because it ought by now to be obvious that our romantic emphasis on "heroism"—as opposed to everyday, steadfast, unassuming courage—is an elemental part of the American love affair with death. A television script writer can become a success with a vocabulary of fifty words or less ("Code 104!" "Code Blue!" "Police!" "Ten ccs. of sodium bicarb!"), so long as the sound effects include shrieks, groans, thuds, sirens, screeching tires, and plenty of gunfire.

Edmund Kemper behaved responsibly—so far as the record shows—for two years after he was discharged from Atascadero. But when he started killing young women, the nature of these crimes was so heinous and bizarre to a "normal" person that they seem to belong more to a dark phase of pre-history. He was a throwback. Yet he was a product of today.

I turned to the Holy Bible to learn what had so appealed to Kemper in the role of Job, beside his well-known boils. I was enlightened.

Not only did Job's experiences offer the most hallowed and respectable support to young Edmund in his growing feelings of aggressiveness and resentment toward women, for the Christian patriarchs make it abundantly clear that women are unclean, unworthy, and fit only to be treated as chattels, but the role suited him too insofar as Job also had been plagued by the ridicule of children.

In chapter 25 of Job: "How then can man . . . be clean that is born of a woman?"

How indeed? And where did Edmund's mother get off, first defiling her son at birth and then making a career of bossing him around?

Job, making a solemn protestation of his integrity, beseeches God to consider the odds against the vulnerable male: "If mine heart have been deceived by a woman, or if I have laid wait at my neighbour's door; then let my wife grind unto another, and let others bow down upon her. For this is an heinous crime; yeah, it is an iniquity to be punished by the judges."

Bright young Edmund was able to put it together. The only translation for a reasonably intelligent boy to make: If a man commits adultery with the wife of another man, then his own wife, although innocent, shall be raped by every man in the neighborhood, for only then can the husband be properly punished.

This makes sense once you accept the idea that a wife has no life as a human being but only as the chattel of her husband, a view that is still quite widely held in the contemporary world.

If Dr. William Glasser had been writing the Bible he might have singled this out as the beginning of sanctimonious buck-passing; but there it was and remains for every Christian boy to read and to twist this way and that in his impressionable, germinal, semenal thoughts.

And then in chapter 30, Job is violently beset by his childish tormenters: "Among the bushes they brayed; under the nettles they were gathered together. They were the children of fools, yea, children of base men; they were viler than the earth. And now am I their song, yea, I am their byword. They abhor me, they flee far from me, and spare not to spit in my face . . .

"Upon my right hand rise the youth; they push away my feet, and they raise up against me the ways of their destruction . . ."

Huge, left-handed, brilliant Edmund always fled in terror from such pursuers. The Accounts Payable must have started then, or even earlier.

The late anthropologist Gregory Bateson, who described himself as an enlightened atheist, said in another context that the only thing wrong with Job—who was primarily noted for patience and steadfastness under trial—was his piousness.

This writer—from a woman's viewpoint—sees little wrong with Job except for the fact that he would have made a very uncomfortable spouse or neighbor.

Even a humanitarian and civil libertarian as enlightened as Dr. Karl Menninger seemed unable to comprehend the bearing on American violence of sociosexual myth and superstition. The criminal mind makes a very easy transition from scapegoat to victim. To kill a scapegoat is to become a hero.

Dr. Menninger wrote in *Love and Hate*, for example, about a great controversy that arose in New York City in 1922 when a statue called "Civic Virtue" was erected in City Hall Park. It represented a man standing victorious above a heap of conquered temptations in the form of women. For at least two decades this work drew the ire of feminists who resented the suggestion that "man symbolizes virtue and woman vice." The sculptor Frederick W. MacMonnies put it down to mere unreasonable pique at the suggestion that some man had finally found the strength to triumph over "the most widely accepted form of temptation." Dr. Menninger cites the matter to make his point, which appears to be that woman's highest role is to prevent men from becoming "the victims of their own self-destructiveness." (In fairness, he was writing these lines in the dark ages of the 1940's.) The necrophile, incidentally, finds statues a particular source of sexual excitement.

A journalist asked why Kemper had had to "sacrifice" six beautiful young women before he killed his mother—a question which happened to be on many lips, both among medical doctors and laymen—the clear implication being that Clarnell Strandberg more or less deserved killing because her son claimed she was aggressive and domineering (characteristics unquestioningly accepted by the head doctors who had never met her), and because in our patriarchal society mothers traditionally have been blamed for the irresponsibility of their sons, and because, as a woman in her fifties in a youth-oriented society, she no longer commanded much sexual value.

Why, in fact, did Kemper kill the younger women first? It was not necessarily because he found them more sexually exciting than he did his mother, even though they were more physically beautiful. He feared her, while they were natural victims. If he killed his mother she might scold him.

Fromm, in *The Heart of Man*, writes of necrophilia, narcissism, and incestuous fixation, which in their separate, nonmalignant forms, need not cause a grave incapacity for reason or love, or create intense destructiveness. As an example of the moderately mother-fixed, moderately narcissistic, and strongly life-loving person, he cited Franklin D. Roosevelt. And by contrast, Hitler, as "an almost totally necrophilous, narcissistic, and incestuous person." (A number of American presidents, incidentally, have had mothers who were probably as strong and domineering as Kemper's.) The more the three tendencies converge, Fromm says, the more malignment they become. The individual is not free to love others, being absorbed with his mother and himself as one person. When personal narcissism with incest fixation is transformed into group narcissism, the result may be a racial or religious fanatic. In the most archaic forms the symbiosis is joined by necrophilia. Fromm sees the craving to return to the womb and the past as a death-wish.

Wilhelm Stekel's studies (*Sadism and Masochism*) led him to conclude that persons suffering from these disorders have a predominantly "retrospective" orientation toward life that forces them to relive again and again certain early conflict situations through symbolizations, projections, and role exchanges. Fairy tales disclose many examples of cannibalism and necrophilia as a primitive residue, just as remnants of blood sacrifice are found in the various religions. But the familiar cases in literature of necrophiliac, cannibalistic, or vampiristic crime, he found, almost always had to do with mentally diseased individuals or epileptics whose illness was unrecognized. The sadist is subject to horrible fantasies, but in more normal persons, "an unbridgeable chasm yawns between fantasy and reality."

The crucial gulf between fantasy and "acting out" has placed the American Dream under a cloud of suspicion by contemporary behaviorists. Dr. Abrahamsen asks, in *Our Violent Society*, why, since the Oedipus complex is universal, individual violence in the U.S. far exceeds that in other developed countries. A culture that so prizes success, celebrity, affluence, and power, he suggests, intensifies the unresolved Oedipal conflict between father and son for the mother. It is a battle that the son will naturally lose. In a healthy situation he would be able to rise above his loneliness and fear, and in time, find a wife of his own. But if overwhelmed by feelings of helplessness, if cornered, so to speak, by the world, he may well act out his hostile impulses. In Abrahamsen's view, the dominant-mother, weak-or-absent-father situation common in our society may increase a child's feelings of being threatened and powerless. And it is natural that feelings of weakness and hence the need to strike out in violence will predominate among those who are excluded from the U.S. mainstream.

He maintains that in all of what we call senseless or aimless violence, there is a strong sexual element. The small child, because of emotional involvement with the mother at this stage, is likely to perceive sexual intercourse as a sado-masochistic act. Fear and anxiety may be fixed in the childish mind, resulting in distortions that prevent the grown man from seeing the facts of life as they are. To the murderer, his "senseless act" has meaning even when it remains hidden from him.

What motivations from infancy underlay Edmund Kemper's murderous drives we cannot know, and it is highly possible that he does not either, although his very early recollections of associating death with love are significant. For science to be able to delineate the beginnings of his illness could only enhance our understanding of violence and perhaps prove helpful to him. In fact, with his intelligence and more-than-lay knowledge of psychology, his brain unimpaired by drug use, he ought to make an ideal subject for research. But this immediately raises the inflammatory question of whether a convict's civil rights can ever really be protected in an environment of prison research. Which leads to the equally controversial question of whether it is not an infringement of a convict's rights to deny him any benefits that might accrue from such new knowledge.

Shortly after the apprehension of Kemper and two other mass murderers in Santa Cruz, UCSC held a campus seminar on the causes and nature of violence, to which were invited leading criminologists, law enforcement officers, and behavioral scientists—a game effort to find out what might be learned through more intensive research. Among academicians, this of course inferred a follow-up effort to obtain federal funding. At that time both liberals and radicals were apt to regard federal money as likely to be tainted by a Nixon administration notoriously unconcerned about the protection of civil rights. Ironically, radical students stormed the seminar, interrupting speakers, until the conference on violence was broken up in near violence.

The question of *why* serial killing has become an almost uniquely American nightmare is not simply answered. Like many other crimes, it thrives in a fragmented, disruptive, unstable society where children often grow up without hope, with suicidal feelings, and little to lose. Some scientists believe it is a syndrome, a group of symptoms characterizing a disease, which are likely to include brain damage from head beating and a general pattern of childhood neglect and abuse.

"We think of ourselves as a nation that cherishes its children, but in fact, America treats its children like excess baggage," charges economist Sylvia Anne Hewlett. "...our tax code offers greater incentives for breeding horses than for raising children. We slash school budgets and deny working parents the right to spend even a few weeks with their newborns. We spend 23% of the federal budget on the elderly but less than 5% on children. (Time, Aug. 26, 1991)

Spending more billions of dollars on new prisons and larger police forces appears ineffective in reducing crime. The Bureau of Justice Statistics reports that the nation's prison population has risen by almost 134% since 1980. At the end of 1989, 4.1 million adults or about one person in 46 were in correctional custody.

Law enforcement officers, for some reason, often argue for the retention of laws against public drunkenness, loitering, prostitution, and bingo playing, even while protesting that their forces are inadequate to capture robbers, rapists, and murderers. Insofar as Kemper is concerned, once his life had made him a calculating killer, there was little to be done for him short of some radical scientific breakthrough.

Perhaps more important breakthroughs will come in the basic field of human nutrition. Biochemical illnesses resulting from too much refined carbohydrates, too little complex carbohydrates and protein, and widely varying individual needs for vitamins and minerals began in the seventies to command serious scientific attention. Although much remains to be done in terms of controlled experiments, there is hope that the onset of a congeries of diseases—pellagra, hypoglycemia, diabetes, schizophrenia, and addiction to alcohol and drugs—might be forestalled with proper nutrition. And many sufferers are finding diets prescribed by their doctors extremely effective. Such diseases are widespread in the U.S. All, in acute phases, may cause their sufferers to react with anger and aggressiveness, and to experience depression, anxiety, frustration, hallucinations, or unaccountable fears. In short, they are related to the whole range of human neuroses. No one knows how many children in the U.S. with various kinds of problems, including hyperactivism, would respond favorably to improved nutrition.

Dr. Ralph Bolton of Pomona College, California, spent five years studying the Qolla peasants in a mountainous, life-discouraging part of Peru. The Qolla are thought by anthropologists to be the meanest people in the world—two million of them, always spoiling for a fight. When a Qolla says, "I am a man," all other men within hearing range take this to mean that he accuses them of being lacking in manhood, and a terrible brawl ensues at once. It may escalate to war. When not engaged in battle, the Qolla devote their spare time to theft, rape, arson, slander, cheating on debts, fighting over property ownership, and to the garden variety of maiming and homicide. In a village of 1,200 Qolla, Dr. Bolton found that half the heads of household had been involved in homicide cases—not always against their wives. The rate of homicide among the Qolla is 50 per 100,000—considerably higher even than in the U.S.

The Qolla diet is poor. Dr. Bolton did blood sugar tests in one village and discovered that 50 percent of adult males suffered from low blood sugar or hypoglycemia.

He believes the Qolla, in an effort to restore their blood sugar balances, psyche themselves into a state of anger which brings a temporary response from their internal organs. The Eskimo, by comparison, withstands great environmental stress on a diet of fats and protein, with very little carbohydrate. Not only is there no word for *war* in any Eskimo language, but anthropologists have had great difficulty persuading the Eskimo that other peoples actually do march forth to kill perfect strangers.

Blood sugar tests of automobile drivers involved in accidents might well disclose astonishing results. Considering that 49,000 persons died in transportation accidents in 1988, such research seems worth undertaking.

In this work, at any event, we are able to speak with more certitude than before of one outgrowth of our times: the American disease of victimitis. We may look at the socio-sexual milieu in which patriarchal, Orestean crimes are able to feed and grow, titillating the public for a brief headline-burst while bringing in that instant before the criminal's downfall or death, substantial psychic reward.

CHAPTER EIGHTEEN

SOCIOSEXUAL VIOLENCE

THE STACKING OF the deck against Mom has a venerable prebiblical history, originating in legend with the transition from the matriarchal to the patriarchal system in Ancient Greece. Orestes, an Athenian youth, slew his mother to punish her for alleged crimes, thus depriving her of the remedy of trial by jury, and made no bones about it.

"Drawn sword in hand, I gashed her neck."

When the Furies came upon Orestes moping red-handed around the statue of Athena on the Acropolis, he declared that Apollo himself had urged him to kill his mother and that suckling pigs had been sacrificed to cleanse him. What more did they want?

His motivations were that his mother, as he alleged, had committed adultery and thereafter had slain his father, both dishonoring the family and making him an orphan. Orestes, a prime example of the irrational male, had then proceeded to make himself doubly orphaned. Since the dead woman could not be tried, the truth of the son's charges remain historical hearsay.

Twelve citizens of Athens were speedily summoned to hear the case against Orestes.

Apollo himself testified in what he described as a "soothfast word" for the defense, pronouncing that a woman's womb was not the true parent of the child. A woman but nursed the seed sown by the father. Hence the male was sole parent. As proof of this fact of creation, he cited the case of Athena, daughter of Zeus, who never had known the darkness of the womb but sprang full-blown from her father's brow. The line of reasoning was clear: since there had been no mother, how could matricide have been committed? How could it even be a crime?

In modern times the law extends protection to Mom as it does to other human beings, but myth and tradition linger on in the glandular rationalizations of her sons—who, in a confused effort to compensate, deluge her with Hallmark greeting cards and boxes of candy on Mother's Day.

Mother-hatred as in Kemper's case often inspires the seemingly random slaughter of other female scapegoats. As a general rule, a man who blames the handiest, weakest woman for his shortcomings never commits anything more drastic than the little murders of the mind. But these too in extension may exert damaging effects. A child's whole sense of identity in its formative stage is bound up in the image it holds of its parents.

It is not surprising of a culture that nurtures sociosexual violence that modern slang usage contains almost no terms of contempt applicable to the male yet provides a fertile selection of epithets for women. Even when a man is called a son-of-a-bitch or a bastard, the insult is really an accusation that his mother was overly compliant. The commonplace expressions used in manly assessment of the female (broads, dogs, cunts, whores, hookers, bitches, sluts, etc.), especially when fortified by a holy writ that sanctimoniously attests to male virtue and to the corresponding unworthiness of woman, exert a profound influence on the small, malleable minds of disturbed boys. They define the scapegoat.

Thus too the Orestean crime promises to win for the young male killer coveted membership in the adult male longhouse or locker room.

Unfortunately, Apollo's theory that the father should be considered "parent of the child" falls tragically wide of the traditional male assumption of responsibility in contemporary America. A high proportion of households provide no loving father as model for growing boys. In Kemper's case, as with most criminals, the child was a victim before he became a criminal, which is not to absolve the criminal of responsibility. His sisters too were deprived of their natural father. In any event, after the father remarried and a stepson preempted Edmund's place, all contact was broken. The father never visited his son in prison or the hospital and took the trouble to have his address removed from the telephone directory.

Clarnell Strandberg did visit her son in prison and the hospital, did pick up the pieces when the family had to move, raised the other children, accepted Edmund back into the home after his first murders, even though he was then past the age of legal adulthood, worried about him, felt shame, guilt, and fear, yet never denied her role as mother. She was scorned by her son for being middle-aged, female, and not very attractive, was hated by him both for having rejected him as well as for allegedly meddling in his personal life, and ultimately was murdered for her pains. Had Clarnell Strandberg been gifted with foresight, surely "a modest proposal of infanticide" might reasonably have been entertained by her.

In the extensive reporting of the murders, Clarnell was never portrayed as other than logical victim; and never simply as a human being who was enjoying a useful and productive life (with which, incidentally, she had by no means finished).

But even women who are young and attractive tend to be punished by society for falling into the error of victimization. Some theorists feel that the victims of murders are really unimportant in that they seem often to be randomly chosen and therefore can shed little light on crimes of violence. But if it were true that victims did not matter, it would surely be a waste to spend so many millions of dollars seeking the conviction of their predators—except, that is, to satisfy a thirst for vengeance. Still, there is a lingering suspicion that "nice girls don't get murdered," and if they do, they're no longer nice girls, so well . . .

Dr. Abrahamsen is among those who hold that some victims habitually expose themselves to violence. He believes that indiscriminate seductiveness in men and women is a typical victim's trait. And he has enraged today's feminists by expressing the hope that the courts, in determining a criminal's sentence, will consider the victim's behavior—a gratuitous wish in the case of rape, as extremely low conviction rates amply demonstrate.

Anglo-Saxon law, by tenaciously reenforcing the male view of woman as chattel—even after enlightened men had been liberated from it—resulted in such feminist *causes célebres* as the California case of Inez Garcia in which the law made a criminal of the alleged primary victim. Garcia was convicted of the second-degree murder of one of the two men she charged had participated in raping her, and was sent to prison, while one of her alleged rapists presumably is enjoying his freedom. The superior court judge hearing her case rigorously forbade any evidence of rape to be introduced, declaring that the only matter to be considered was the charge of murder.

But public attitudes, those of police departments, and even the laws of some states are changing, to bring a promise of equity. JoAnn Little, black, aged twenty, was early acquitted of the first-degree murder of a guard she alleged sexually attacked her when she was held as the only female prisoner in the Beaufort County, North Carolina jail. Had she been convicted, she would have received the death penalty.

It is no doubt natural that some men have difficulty understanding that a woman's body is her own property, since a few women themselves still seem unable to grasp the concept. After all, a woman traditionally is signed over in a marriage in which her father ceremoniously transfers title to her—at her own wish, yet under heavy social pressure to conform. This event usually occurs only a few years after she has ceased to be a minor. Thus victimitis, although it is essentially a disease of impaired ego, is firmly rooted in institutions.

Those who are weak or who command the least status are most often victimized. Millions of incidents are reported in the U.S. each year of brutal child battering, many of which are fatal. And such gross physical abuse often becomes a part of the childhood history of future criminal psychopaths. The highest percentage of "family" murders involve men murdering their common-law wives, victims of little social status or recourse.

Victims—for whatever reasons—*are* often repeaters, in the same way that criminals are. One New York girl, Dolores Perez, 22, had been mugged six times, which she put down to the fact that she was quite small, a woman, and lived in a high-crime area. But her friends, she told *Newsweek*, assumed she was taking stupid risks and that she must have been unconsciously seeking or provoking the attacks.

Dr. Martin Symonds, an associate professor of psychiatry at New York University School of Medicine, has studied hundreds of victims of violent crime and finds that they are often tormented by long-term anxiety and guilt. In this reaction they are quite justified, he says, because of the peculiarly negative attitudes of many people toward them. If the public can somehow transfer to a victim the blame for seemingly irrational and random violence, it helps everyone to feel less vulnerable.

An enlightened public attitude toward victims and most of all, greater understanding by law enforcement personnel who are usually first on the scene, could alleviate the most damaging psychological after-effects of personal aggression.

Hitchhikers of both sexes are easily the most obvious, continuing, "invitational" victims. In California nowadays, most hitchhikers tend to pair up—not that such a precaution ever stopped a killer like Kemper.

He of course was quite right in pointing out that the girls he killed were "asking for it" by ignoring the dangers of a jungle that even he found threatening; and it must be admitted that his authority was indisputable.

As violence becomes more and more accepted in the United States, our definition of "normal behavior" is being inexorably changed. What is acceptable savagery for us is not normal for Canadians just across the border. The law is a society's way of defining and ordering conduct. Either we learn to control our violent behavior or we revise our law to accommodate the changing "norms." Our judicial system will cease to command much respect if we do not act to correct the disparity between what is socially acceptable and what is lawful.

The view is widespread that a person who could commit the series of brutal and bizarre crimes that Edmund Kemper committed, undeterred by any tinge of normal human empathy for the victims and their families, boasting even of his efficiency as a mass killer, *had* to be crazy. The law says that a killer who calculated his acts so intelligently and carefully *had* to be sane. He is diagnosed as a sociopath. This, in jurisprudent application, is not to be mistaken as signifying mental illness, brain damage, genetic impairment, catathymic crisis, or any other kind or cause of derangement qualifying as "legal" insanity. Next year perhaps even the term *sociopath* will be regarded as too stigmatizing and a mass murderer will simply be described as an "over-achiever." But not even that for long. It has become relatively common in recent years for juvenile criminals who commit particularly heinous crimes— sometimes emulating the exact method of murder depicted in a recent TV program or movie—to demonstrate an insensibility and indifference that baffles psychiatrists, since they can find no sense of guilt from which to work. Often such criminals were brutalized as young children and have spent their entire lives in a depressed environment. They are a very normal product of a slum. In assessing where they stand in relation to *their* world, they are eminently sane.

For forty years, the United States has led all developed countries in the dubious distinction of having the highest rate of violent crimes. Perhaps it is not unrelated that it has led the world in much else too, notably in material wealth, the swiftness of technological change, and the reverence of power. Sharp economic disparities between classes in a socially mobile, democratic country undoubtedly work as a strong abrasive favoring criminal behavior.

Violent crime in the U.S. has been increasing faster than the population—almost ten times as fast. It rose 203.8 percent between 1960 and 1973. Rape jumped 165 percent in fifteen years.

Uniform Crime Reports, 1990, disclose on average one property crime every two seconds, one murder every 22 minutes, one forcible rape every 5 minutes (and most rapes still go unreported).

Another source reports that one woman is battered in domestic crime every 13 seconds. And in 1991, the Bureau of Justice Statistics disclosed that each year from 1985 to 1988, boys and girls 12 to 19 were victims of 1.9 million rapes, robberies, and assaults. Of every 1,000 American teenagers, 67 experienced violent crimes during those years—half of which occurred in school buildings, on school property, or on the streets.

Homicide rates here are about ten times those of the Scandinavian countries. Manhattan, with a population of 1.5 million, has more murders annually than the entire United Kingdom, with a population of 60 million.

In Toronto, Canada, a huge metropolis of many distinctive ethnic districts, but without slums comparable to America's, forty-five persons were murdered in 1973. Natives claimed that crime was less of a problem than frost. Only a few miles away in the great industrial city of Detroit, however, 860 persons were murdered that year, a rate of 19.3 per 100,000.

Ordinary visitors from Toronto explain their low rate of violent crime by saying that they are simply not uptight, not as competitive as Americans, feel less crowded and driven. They dislike the success-oriented Americanization they feel encroaching on Canadian culture through physical proximity and multinational industry. On the other hand, a young Torontonian I talked with in Berkeley said he found the sheer energy radiating from street people and students milling along Telegraph Avenue unlike anything at home; and it was clear that he found it exciting, although he wouldn't want to live there.

The American Dream, the more we scrutinize it, seems inseparable from the violence which, in its own way, beguiles us all. We the public, who merely feed on violence, develop a mechanism that is somewhat similar to a murderer's. To move from fantasies of crime to their acting out is for the criminal a great, great step. For the public, the process is reversed. We develop a mechanism that permits us to move backward from the reality of crime to the pretense that it is merely an art form provided for our escape reading and escape viewing. The very fact that this book is being read is largely the result of

Kemper's meticulously detailed accounts of his assaults upon dead and dying human beings. Still we do not wish to admit that persons such as he exist, that we may be their next victim, or that a child or friend or dear relative may be. But displace this feeling into the realm of play-acting, and we become willing voyeurs.

Unfortunately there are too many in this volatile society for whom the play is mightily infectious. The portrayal of sadism is contagious for weak and frustrated persons.

While it is difficult to feel any sympathy for a Kemper, who proved himself capable of executing in cold blood any horror of which his fertile mind could conceive with precious little remorse, I nevertheless could not help but conclude that he too was one more victim. Regardless of the medical experts' reluctance to so testify, it seemed likely that, outside of a rigidly controlled environment, he could not avoid the cyclical build-up of tensions that created an inexorable need to kill, and that his killings therefore were the product of a diseased mind. Yet he certainly knew the difference between right and wrong.

Laws and institutions—even commercial television programming—can be changed. Teenaged girls can be taught self-defense in the public schools, with the explicit goal of educating them to cease being victims and to cease thinking like second-class citizens. Even sexism can be abolished and men liberated from its crushing pressures.

But a retracing of violence always leads back to the hearth and home, if any. We shall never correct the underlying sickness until, as parents and adults, we can actually, physically feel how our words and actions react in the mind of a child. An effective way to kill mosquito larvae in a pond is to pour kerosene on the surface. It forms a suffocating film. Sometimes we treat our children as if they were mosquito larvae in a pond; but most of them, unlike such insects, do not die; they merely adapt, many in damaged form, and live to breed another generation.

Printed in the United States
31291LVS00005B/162

9 780595 089154